Developing A Christian Apologetics Educational Program

Developing A Christian Apologetics Educational Program

In the Secondary School

DOUGLAS E. POTTER

WIPF & STOCK · Eugene, Oregon

DEVELOPING A CHRISTIAN APOLOGETICS EDUCATIONAL PROGRAM
In the Secondary School

Wipf & Stock
An Imprint of Wipf and Stock Publishers
199 W. 8th Ave., Suite 3
Eugene, OR 97401
www.wipfandstock.com

ISBN 13: 978-1-55635-503-5

Manufactured in the U.S.A.

To my beloved daughter
Allison

Contents

List of Illustrations ix
Introduction xi

1 A BRIEF HISTORY OF APLOGETICS 1
   Apologetics in the New Testament • Early Church Fathers •
   Middle Ages • Reformation • Modern • Contemporary

2 APOLOGETIC SYSTEMS 20
   Classical • Evidential • Experiential • Presuppositional •
   Combinational • A Defense of the Classical Approach •
   Educational Reasons for Classical Apologetics • History and the
   Classification of Apologetics

3 THE CASE FOR CHRISTIAN APLOGETICS EDUCATION
      IN THE SECONDARY SCHOOL 38
   A Contemporary Need • Educational Value of Apologetics at
   the Secondary School Level • Appropriateness of Apologetics in
   the Secondary School • Answering Some Objections

4 WORD VIEWS AND CHRISTIAN EDUCATION 58
   God's Revelation • Educational World Views • Apologetics and
   Christian World View Education

5 TOWARD A PHILOSOPHY OF CHRISTIAN EDUCATION
      FOR APOLOGETICS: GENERAL REVELATION 68
   Truth • Metaphysics • Epistemology • Natural Theology •
   Science • History • Education

6 TOWARD A PHILOSOPHY OF CHRSITAIN EDUCATION
      FOR APOLOGETICS: SPECIAL REVELATION 94
   Biblical Inspiration • Biblical Interpretation • The Holy Spirit
   and Apologetics Education • Christian Education • Christian
   Apologetics Education

7 A Curriculum Model for Christian Apologetics
        Education 105

The Nature of Curriculum • Christian Education Curriculum •
The Nature of Apologetics as a Subject of Study

8 Curriculum Materials Needed for Christian
        Apologetics Education 124

Introduction to the Curriculum • Goals of Christian Apologetics
Education • Instructional Analysis of Christian Apologetics
Education • Interdisciplinary Nature of Apologetics

9 The Future of Christian Apologetics Education 151

Appendix A   Research on Christian Apologetics Education
                    in the Secondary School 155
Teaching the Subject of Christian Apologetics • Grade Levels of
Instruction in Christian Apologetics • Christian Apologetics as
a Distinct Subject of Study • Length of Instruction Offered in
Christian Apologetics • Teachers with a Degree in the Subject
• Teacher Training in Christian Apologetics • Method of
Christian Apologetics • Years Teaching Christian Apologetics
• Curriculum Materials Used for Christian Apologetics •
Limitations and Conclusions of the Study

Appendix B   Sample Unit 170
Appendix C   An Argument for Christianity 201
Bibliography 203

List of Illustrations

Figure 1.1 Apologetics as the Foundation of Theology 14
Table 1.1 Apologetic Systems through History 18
Table 2.1 Presuppositionalism Compared 27
Table 2.2 Persons and Apologetic Systems 36
Table 3.1 Growth of Religions in the U.S. 41
Figure 4.1 Development of Educational Philosophy 59
Figure 4.2 Relationship between General and Special Revelation 60
Table 4.1 Educational World Views Compared 63–64
Figure 5.1 Vertical and Horizontal Cosmological Arguments Compared 79
Figure 5.2 Relationship of Schooling-Education-Learning 87
Table 5.1 Authoritarian and Non-authoritarian Philosophies Compared 81
Figure 7.1 Curriculum Domains 108
Figure 7.2 Taxonomy for the Acquisition of Organized Knowledge 109
Figure 7.3 Taxonomy for Biblical Studies 110
Figure 7.4 Tasks of Apologetics 114
Table 7.1 Flesch Readability Test 117
Table 7.2 Apologetics Textbook Analysis Chart 121
Table 8.1 Apologetics Semester Schedule 127
Table 8.2 Basic Interdisciplinary Skills Chart 146

Introduction

THIS BOOK IS FOR those interested in teaching Christian apologetics as a formal subject of study especially at the secondary school level. You may already be a Christian apologist, Christian educator, director, pastor, Bible teacher, or a homeschool parent, but when it comes to understanding apologetics as it relates to education, or fitting the subject into the curriculum you are not quite sure where to begin, how to justify it, or what to include to make the program successful. This is a guide or supplemental text to developing a Christian education curriculum that incorporates apologetics as a distinct subject of study. Most texts dealing with Christian education or apologetics do not directly address the implementation or teaching of apologetics as a subject. Hence, this book would be appropriate as a supplement to either a class on Christian education or apologetic ministry.

Certainly, the subject and study of Christian Apologetics is not new. What is new is where and perhaps how it is being taught. Prior to the 1990s few secondary Christian schools incorporated apologetics as a subject of study. Even if they did, it was probably only as an integrated subject of study in other disciplines. Since then, however, a growing number of Christian schools have chosen to add apologetics and more have decided to teach it as a distinct subject of study.[1] It is interesting to note that the same kind of change has occurred in higher education particularly at the seminary level. Prior to the 1990s, it would have been difficult finding any Seminary in the U. S. that offered a graduate degree with a concentration in Christian apologetics. That is changing since many Christian educators at various levels of education are coming to realize the importance of the subject. I have formally studied education and have professionally taught in both Christian and non-Christian high schools. Over the past sixteen years, I have studied the subject of apolo-

1. See appendix A for research concerning the subject of apologetics in the Christian secondary school. All statistics regarding apologetics in Christian secondary institutional schools cited in this book are taken from this research project.

getics and for nine of those years I have worked in a higher educational institution that specializes in apologetics. Over these years, I have spoken with numerous Christian teachers and administrators. My experience has brought me to the conclusion that there is a serious gap between the apologist and the typical Christian educator. What seems to be lacking is the ability of educators and apologists to combine their knowledge and skills. Much of what is labeled, or thought to be apologetics in the Christian schools is not. Many educators find themselves in a quandary when trying to understand the vast complexity of different apologetic arguments and systems. Likewise, many schooled in the disciplines of theology and apologetics have little exposure to the process and methods of education especially at the secondary school level. This present work is an attempt to provide a solution by suggesting a framework for developing a Christian Apologetics Educational (CAE) program that is specific to the needs of a secondary school environment.

To accomplish this, nine chapters cover relevant material. First, a brief history of apologetics is discussed for exposing the educator to the continual effort of major Christian thinkers that defend the Faith (Chapter 1). Second, various systems of apologetics are presented and examined in order to conclude which system is most appropriate for a CAE program (Chapter 2). Third, a justification is made for implementing apologetics as a subject of study at the secondary school level (Chapter 3). Fourth, the nature of God's revelation is provided to study the subjects of education and apologetics (Chapter 4). Fifth, elements of a philosophy of education are suggested to support a Christian approach to apologetics education (Chapter 5 and 6). Sixth, a conceptual framework and model is developed for a CAE curriculum (Chapter 7). Seventh, curriculum materials needed such as outlines, guides, goals, and instructional objectives are presented (Chapter 8). Finally, a look towards the future of Christian apologetics education is offered (Chapter 9).We have also included some appendices that give some statistical data concerning apologetics in Christian schools (Appendix A), a sample curriculum unit (Appendix B), and an overall argument for the Christian faith (Appendix C).

The chapters work together to provide a thorough justification to properly understand and implement a CAE program. Effort is made to present concepts simply and clearly so both the educator and apologist can combine their knowledge and incorporate apologetics and teacher educational materials.

The trial ground work for this was a series of lessons given at Grace Bible Church, Charlotte, North Carolina, as part of the Doctor of Ministry Seminar titled *Apologetics in Christian Educational Ministry*. Most of the participants in those lessons were parents who homeschooled their children. Therefore, this work has a direct application to parents who desire apologetics to be taught in their home as well as the professional educator that desires it in their school or ministry.

The term "Christian school" or "Christian educator," as used in this work, should be understood to cover both institutional and home-schools. The term "secondary school" should be understood to refer to students in grades 9–12 or 14–18 years old.

I would like especially to thank those that provided assistance, in making recommendations, corrections, and constructive criticism of this work. It is much improved because of their efforts. These include my mentor in apologetics and theology Dr. Norman L. Geisler and Christian education Dr. Barry R. Leventhal. I would also like to thank my teachers in philosophy Dr. Richard G. Howe and biblical studies Dr. Thomas A. Howe. I of course, assume full responsibility for any errors. I want also to acknowledge my father, Ray Potter, who greatly helped in reviewing this work and most of all, my wife Wendy whose unending love and support made this book possible.

A Brief History of Apologetics

OBJECTIVES

Identify significant apologists and the issues on which they wrote.

Trace the development of apologetics as a practice and subject of study.

M OST SUBJECTS STUDIED IN school have a history to which it is worth exposing even the beginning student. Apologetics is no different. This brief survey of a history of apologetics covers some of the major apologists since the beginning of Christianity. After reading this chapter, you should gain an appreciation for the intellectual challenges faced historically by these thinkers and the individuals that responded to such challenges. The approach is positive, as opposed to being overly critical. No analysis is made of the ultimate value of each contribution to the field of apologetics. Instead, focus is directed to the subject of apologetics itself as an enduring subject with a distinctive history. It is also hoped that you will be convinced that a subject with such a central role in Christianity should be important to the development of any Christian educational curriculum.

APOLOGETICS IN THE NEW TESTAMENT

While no book in the New Testament should be considered an apologetic treatise, almost every book includes some elements that can be considered apologetic[1] in some sense. Catholic historian Avery Dulles

1. The word apologetics comes from the Greek words *apologeomai* and *apologia*. In the New Testament it concerns a defense in the form of a speech or some kind of reply.

concurs by stating in his history of apologetics that, "None of the New Testament writings is directly and profusely apologetical, nearly all of them contain reflections of the Church's efforts to exhibit the credibility of its message and to answer the obvious objections that would have arisen in the minds of adversaries, prospective converts, and candid believers."[2] We begin with some clear imperatives in the New Testament given to believers concerning apologetics.

A Biblical Imperative

The Apostle Paul, in one of the most apologetic of his works, encourages believers in the face of an insipient form of Gnosticism not to only answer everyone, but to know how to do so. "Be wise in the way you act toward outsiders; make the most of every opportunity. Let your conversation be always full of grace, seasoned with salt, so that you may know how to answer everyone" (Col 4:5–6). In 2 Corinthians, Paul asserts to a morally wayward church questioning his apostleship, that his goal is to "demolish arguments and every pretension that sets itself up against the knowledge of God, and we take captive every thought to make it obedient to Christ" (2 Cor 10:5). Paul describes to Titus an essential quality that must be found in a church leader: "He must hold firmly to the trustworthy message as it has been taught, so that he can encourage others by sound doctrine and refute those who oppose it" (Titus 1:9). He further elaborates to Timothy how to handle those that might oppose leadership in the church. "The Lord's servant must not quarrel; instead, he must be kind to everyone, able to teach, not resentful. Those who oppose him, he must gently instruct, in the hope that God will grant them repentance leading them to a knowledge of the truth" (2 Tim 2:24–25). Under house arrest in Rome, Paul writes to a church at Philippi describing what his mission has been and continues to be: "It is right for me to feel this way about all of you, since I have you in my heart; for whether I am in chains or defending and confirming the gospel, all of you share in God's grace with me. . . . The latter do so in love, knowing that I am put here for the defense of the gospel" (Phil 1:7, 16). Peter, likewise, provides one of the clearest encouragements and imperatives for Christians who were likely to face persecution. Whether asked to do so formally or informally, he

---

Arndt and Gingrich, *A Greek-English Lexicon of the New Testament*, 95–96.

2. Dulles, *A History of Apologetics*, 23–24.

told them to defend the faith by giving an answer to anyone that asks. "But in your hearts set apart Christ as Lord. Always be prepared to give an answer to everyone who asks you to give the reason for the hope that you have. But do this with gentleness and respect" (1 Pet 3:15). Jude supplies an important imperative that clearly implies a contention for "the faith" that is systematic, complete, or exhaustive. "Dear friends, although I was very eager to write to you about the salvation we share, I felt I had to write and urge you to contend for the faith that was once for all entrusted to the saints" (Jude 3). Here "faith" is understood to be a complete and certain body of knowledge. This being the case, only an apologetic that covers every aspect of the faith will suffice to achieve Jude's goal of contention. Finally, Jesus himself instructs his disciples to: "Love the Lord your God with all your heart and with all your soul and with all your mind" (Matt 22:37). It would hardly be possible to fulfill this command by ignoring objections to the Christian faith. One must use their mind to love God and this implies an honest response that is fully convinced that the Christian faith is true and demonstrably so.

Apostle Paul

The Apostle Paul (1–10–65/67 A.D.), originally known as Saul, was born in Tarsus sometime in the first decade of the Christian era. He was born a Jew of the tribe of Benjamin but also had the privilege of Roman citizenship. Around the age of thirteen he was sent to Jerusalem to study. Eventually he studied under Gamaliel and became a Pharisee equally fluent in Aramaic and Greek. Upon seeing the risen Christ on the road to Damascus, he converted to Christianity (33 A.D.) and spent his early years as a believer in Syria, Arabia, and Judea. Later he embarked on at least three missionary journeys where he started, visited, and wrote letters to various churches.

Luke, who describes much of the Apostle's apologetic activities, begins his Gospel with a description, that clearly portrays a first century defense of his research: "Inasmuch as many have taken in hand to set in order a narrative of those things which have been fulfilled among us, just as those who from the beginning were eyewitnesses and ministers of the word delivered them to us, it seemed good to me also having had perfect understanding of all things from the very first, to write to you an orderly account . . ." (Luke 1:1–3). Luke in the second volume of his Gospel (Acts) reveals opposition that was found among non-Jews (Gentiles). Paul delivers speeches to both Jews and Gentiles as an apologetic. In Acts 17, the regular practice of Paul is described: "Then Paul, *as his custom was*, went in to them [Jews], and for three Sabbaths *reasoned* with them from the Scriptures explaining and demonstrating that the Christ had to suffer and rise again from the dead" (Acts 17:2–3, emphasis added).

In one of the more interesting encounters, Luke describes Paul's encounter with Hellenistic philosophers. The Stoic and Epicurean philosophers could be compared to the beliefs of modern day Atheists and Pantheists respectively. Paul, as analyzed by apologist and author Dr. Kenneth Boa, seems to be arguing in classic Stoic fashion:

> Essentially, the point of this first and longest part of the speech is that idolatry is foolish and that the Stoics themselves have admitted as much, though they had failed to abandon it completely. Paul uses this inconsistency in Stoic philosophy to illustrate the Athenians' ignorance of God. . . . Having proved his major premise, Paul then announces that God has declared an end to ignorance of His nature and will be revealing Himself. Paul concludes that the Resurrection is proof of God's intention to judge the world through Jesus Christ.[3]

The results of this argument are described in exhaustive terms: Some believed, some scoffed, and some expressed further interest.

Paul's writings display a number of apologetic features that are directed mainly against Judaism, Hellenism, and early Gnosticism. Paul's apologetic is grounded in what can be termed general revelation. He asserts in Romans: "That which is known about God is evident within them; for God made it evident to them. For since the creation of the world His invisible attributes, His eternal power and divine nature, have been clearly seen, being understood through what has been made, so that they are without excuse. For even though they knew God, they did not honor Him as God . . ." (1:19–21). All humans "knew God" (v. 21a). By this Paul is implying that all humans have access to some knowledge of God (existence and attributes). Most, however, suppress or subvert this knowledge into idolatrous religious expressions. But Paul's acknowledgement of this knowledge in all humans is a clear acceptance that common universal ground exists in which appeal to reason can be made. Paul expresses a moral reason in chapter 2 (vv. 12–16) stating "that they show the work of the Law written in their hearts, their conscience

3. Boa and Bowman, *Faith has its Reasons*, 26.

bearing witness . . ." (Rom 2:15). Hence, there is a moral law within. As Professor Russ Bush indicates Paul's methodology is first to ground his approach in "theism cosmologically and having pressed the moral implications implicit in this worldview, Paul then turns to the fundamental reality of divine revelation. If there is a God, and if a moral law has been revealed, then it may be cogently argued that divine revelation exists."[4] This is clearly Paul's method and practice as recorded in Acts 17. When Paul faced Jews in the synagogues, who already had prior acceptance of an authoritative Old Testament, he made his argument for Jesus Christ from Scripture but when he faced a non-theistic or Pantheistic audience he started with the reality of God (Acts 17:2, 3. cf. 17:16ff.).

EARLY CHURCH FATHERS

Challenges to the Christian faith did not stop after completion of the New Testament. If anything, challenges intensified from sources such as Judaism, Gnosticism, Paganism, and Hellenistic philosophy. Second and third century apologists modeled their arguments after Hellenistic Jews in order to refute polytheism and paganism. Christians read their writings and probably used them as sources for instruction in theology and apologetics. Historian Eugene Magevney comments on the first one hundred years of early Christian education that, "the matter of instruction was always confined to the doctrines of faith, and was treated catechetically or apologetically, and beyond this neither the first schools at Alexandria or elsewhere seem to have gone." [5] The school at Alexandria likely involved children and covered other fields such as pagan research, science, and literature. Because of the school in Alexandria, by the third century, Magevney tells us there "was a period of marvelous growth and activity in the church, and the almost instantaneous creation of a generation of apologists and controversialists hardly equaled . . . ."[6] Two major apologists representative of this time period are Justin Martyr (ca. 100–165 A.D.) and Origen (ca. 185–254 A.D.).

4. Bush, *A Handbook for Christian Philosophy*, 114.

5. Magevney, *Christian Education in the First Centuries*, 21.

6. Ibid., 33.

Justin Martyr

Justin Martyr converted to Christianity from a Platonistic philosophy. His first apologetic work, *Dialogue with Trypho the Jew*, argued from Hebrew Scriptures that Jesus is the Messiah. After that he completed two *Apologies*. In these works, Justin refuted common errs about Christians being atheistic. In the backdrop of Roman polytheism, Christians appeared to believe in no gods. Actually, as Justin noted, Christians believe in the one and only true God. He further corrected misunderstandings surrounding Christian practices such as taking communion. This was falsely viewed as cannibalistic because of the symbolic representation of the body and blood of Jesus.

In citing the story of Socrates, Justin affirmed the possibility of arriving at the existence of God based on human reason, "he [Socrates] exhorted them to become acquainted with the God who was to them unknown, by means of the investigation of reason."[7] God's existence, according to Justin, was more easily known by means of revelation.

Justin also argued, in the face of Paganism, that Christianity was a morally superior religion and offered prophecy as the basis for belief in Jesus Christ and his resurrection. He summarized his argument at one point by stating: "whatever we assert in conformity with what has been taught us by Christ and by the prophets who preceded Him, are alone true . . . not because we say the same things as these writers said, but because we say true things."[8]

Origen

Origen came from a largely Greek philosophical background. Regrettably Origen espoused many heretical doctrines. Yet, his main apologetic work is perhaps the best from this period. It concerns a response to a Jewish intellectual named Celsus. Origen's work, *Contra Celsum* (*Against Celsus*), argued against Celsus' arguments point by point. He argued against Celsus that Jesus used sorcery or that his miracles were mythical. He further argued for Jesus' historical resurrection. Origen, in response, countered an early version of a hallucination theory to explain Jesus appearances to the Apostles after his resurrection. Their lives and testimony is presented as solid proof: "But a clear and unmistak-

---

7. Justin Martyr, *The Second Apology of Justin*, 10.
8. Justin Martyr, *The First Apology of Justin*, 13.

able proof of the fact [resurrection] I hold to be the undertaking of His disciples, who devoted themselves to the teaching of a doctrine which was attended with danger to human life,—a doctrine which they would not have taught with such courage had they invented the resurrection of Jesus from the dead; and who also, at the same time, not only prepared others to despise death, but were themselves the first to manifest their disregard for its terrors."[9]

Apologetics in the early church is characteristic of a reactionary approach. An objection or argument is made against Christianity, and then certain Christian thinkers formulate and write a response. This would change over time to a more systematic effort that involved an attempt to answering all objections to the Christian faith.

MIDDLE AGES

The Middle Ages saw several great thinkers arise to defend and explain the Christian faith. Three such thinkers, Augustine (354–430), Anselm (1033–1109), and Aquinas (1224/5–1274), contributed immensely to the subject of Apologetics.

Augustine

Augustine is considered one of the greatest Christian thinkers of the First Millennium. With over one hundred books to his credit, he wrote on many subjects in the areas of human culture, philosophy, history, and theology. Many of his works touch on subjects related to apologetics. His most significant apologetic work, *City of God*, refuted Paganism, heresies, and defended Christian truth.

He is the first significant thinker to address the delicate interaction of faith and reason. These two aspects, he believed, played an interactive role in coming to know God through Jesus Christ. He acknowledged that a person may come to faith first, but reason is prior in reality and can help one understand. This understanding allowed Augustine to embrace arguments for God's existence.[10] He reasoned on the same common ground, general revelation, which Paul acknowledged in the New Testament. In the *City of God*, he says, "For, though the voices of

---

9. Origen, "Against Celsus," 114–15.

10. Such arguments are usually classified as cosmological (from creation), teleological (from design), ontological (from being), and axiological (from morality).

the prophets were silent, the world itself, by its well-ordered changes and movements, and by the fair appearance of all visible things, bears a testimony of its own, both that it has been created, and also that it could not have been created save by God, whose greatness and beauty are unutterable and invisible."[11] He also gave arguments for Jesus that included evidence from fulfilled prophecy, miracles from the Bible, mass Christian conversions, and subsequent faith of martyrs. These, he felt, were sufficient to respond to antagonists of the Christian faith. He once commented, "They are much deceived, who think that we believe in Christ without any proofs concerning Christ."[12]

Anselm

Following in Augustine's lead on faith and reason, Anselm brought them together in a two step approach. Anselm asserted, "For I do not seek to understand that I may believe, but I believe in order to understand."[13] To understand the Christian faith, Anselm, authored three books. The first work, *Proslogion*, presents his famous ontological argument. God, he reasoned, is by definition the greatest conceivable being. It would be greater for God to exist in reality than as an idea only in one's mind. Hence, God must really exist in reality or he would not be the greatest conceivable being. While this argument has been severely critiqued, certain forms have survived and play an important definitional role in other more sound arguments. A second work, Anselm's *Monologion*, presented a cosmological type argument from goodness and being (existence). The last work, *Why the God-man* (*Cur Deus Homo*), defends the reasonableness of belief in the deity of Jesus Christ. He uses some of the same traditional arguments found in Augustine's works, but emphasizes the importance of not placing faith on arguments themselves, but in the God-man himself.

Aquinas

By the twelve hundreds, a rediscovery and translation of Aristotle's work had a great impact on Christianity. Averroes, a Spanish-Arab philosopher, provided an understanding of Aristotle that ranged from uncritical

---

11. Augustine, *City of God*, 11.4.
12. Augustine, *Concerning Faith of Things Not Seen*, 5.
13. Anselm, *Proslogium*, 1.

acceptance to outright condemnation by Christians. Albert the Great was the first to provide a significant response to Averroes. But it was his student, Thomas Aquinas, that provided some of the most rigorous and systematic reasoning for the Christian faith.

Aquinas quickly established himself as a major Christian thinker with the *Summa contra Gentiles* that answered the Greco-Arabic world view (i.e., Muslim). He pointedly states the apologetic problem this work must meet: "Thus, against the Jews we are able to argue by means of the Old Testament, while against heretics we are able to argue by means of the New Testament. But the Mohammedans and the pagans accept neither the one nor the other. We must, therefore, have recourse to the natural reason, to which all men are forced to give their assent."[14] His method was skillfully to weave Aristotelian philosophy with and without compromising revealed Christian truth. In his works, Aquinas, explained that there were some truths only discovered by reason and others only known by faith. For example, the existence of God is discoverable by reason. But the truth that God is a triune being is known only by faith. In his own words: "Some truths about God exceed all the ability of the human reason. Such is the truth that God is triune. But there are some truths, which the natural reason also is able to reach. Such are that God exists, that He is one, and the like. In fact, such truths about God have been proved demonstratively by the philosophers, guided by the light of the natural reason."[15] Aquinas' objective was to prove *that* God exists. Such a proof, however, was never expected to make someone have faith *in* God. This was a persuasive task left to the Holy Spirit.

Some apologetic historians have described the result of his labors as a "comprehensive systematic exposition"[16] of Christian Theology that integrated relevant philosophical concerns. His *Summa Theologia*, intended to be an introductory text for beginning medieval theology students, remained unfinished upon his death. His arguments for God's existence, called the Five Ways, are based on First Principles that are grounded in reality. He argued from motion to an Unmoved Mover, from effect to a First Cause, from contingent being to a Necessary Being, from degrees of perfection to a Most Perfect Being, and from design to a Designer. The first four are cosmological type arguments and the last is

14. Aquinas, *Summa Contra Gentiles*, 1.2.3.

15. Ibid., 1.3.2.

16. Reid, *Christian Apologetics*, 111.

teleological. Aquinas also engaged in the traditional evidences of proving the historical truth of Christianity by appealing to fulfilled prophecy, miracles, and mass conversions.

REFORMATION

The Reformation period saw the rise of individuals that desired to reform the Roman Catholic Church. Hence, most of the "apologetic" activity was theological in nature and directed towards reforming the established Roman Catholic Church. However, it is worth noting that the two major Reformers never dismissed the idea of establishing God's existence by the use of human reason. Martin Luther (1483–1564), an Augustinian monk, condemned reason only in the context of it being used to earn merit towards God. While Luther did not develop a formal apologetic, his close associate, Philipp Melanchthon (1497–1560) did. Melanchthon's later edition (1536) of *Loci communes*, contained a formal apologetic that understood philosophy as preparatory in leading men to the gospel. As Dulles observes, "He came to hold that reason could establish without the aid of revelation that God exists; that He is eternal, wise, truthful, just, pure, and beneficent; that He created the world, conserved all things in existence, and punished the wicked."[17] His apologetic position has had a lasting influence in Lutheranism.

John Calvin (1509–1564) considered faith itself reasonable. He admitted that at times, it might seem unreasonable, but this was usually due to spiritual dullness or sin. Calvin fully agreed with the notion of general revelation that manifests God in nature and in the consciousness of men. While Calvin did not elaborate on arguments for God's existence he did allude to them in general. Calvin acknowledged that "[God] manifest his perfections in the whole structure of the universe . . ."[18] and that "it is plain that the Lord has furnished every man with abundant proofs of his wisdom."[19] He also leveled his own arguments for the inspiration of the Bible. Specifically, Calvin addressed these reasons in the *Institutes* in chapter eight of book one titled, "The Credibility of Scripture Sufficiently Proved, in so Far as Natural Reason Admits." Here,

17. See Dulles, *History*, 147.

18. Calvin, *Institutes of the Christian Religion*, 1.5.1. See also Kantzer, "John Calvin's Theory of the Knowledge of God and the Word of God," for an explanation of this view.

19. Ibid., 1.5.2.

and elsewhere, he argues for the Scriptures unity, majesty, prophecies, and miracles. Fredric Howe, commenting on Calvin's apologetic states, "According to Calvin, . . . there is on the one hand a pattern for argumentation and for presenting reasons for the dignity and majesty of Scripture as well as for its entire Christian theistic system."[20]

MODERN

While the concern in the middle ages was knowledge of God, the concern in the modern period was on scientific knowledge. With the beginnings of the enlightenment, intellectuals adopted a starting point that centered on human reasoning to the exclusion of special revelation from God. Advancements in scientific and technological discoveries reinforced a belief that humans could solve physical as well as philosophical problems apart from appeal to theology and traditional Christian doctrine. God was removed from the equation and Deism, the belief that granted God his transcendence but denied his direct involvement (i.e., miracles), was the result.

Anticipating the rise of Deism one important contribution, especially to educational apologetics, was that of Hugo Grotus (1583–1645) who published what many consider the first Protestant text on apologetics. Published in Latin in 1627 and translated into other languages, including English, it was divided into six books. These covered God's existence and nature, evidence for Jesus' life and deity, authority of the New Testament, and a defense against other religions with special attention given to Judaism and Islam. The work was quite popular and stayed in print into the 1800s.[21]

Two Christians rose to the challenge of intellectual Deists: Blaise Pascal (1623–1662) and Joseph Butler (1692–1752). Pascal was a French Catholic mathematician who emphasized a personal and relational aspect to Christian reasoning. He did not outright reject arguments for God, but he did oppose their use in apologetics and therefore did not emphasize them. His book for apologetics, *Pensées* (which means thoughts), was never completed, but remains a significant contribution to an existential and somewhat evidential apologetic. Much of his in-

20. Howe, *Challenge and Response*, 115.
21. Grotius, *The Truth of the Christian Religion*.

fluence was overshadowed by major discoveries in science provided by Newton and Galileo.

Joseph Butler directly confronted the belief of Deists by using an argument of analogy. He reasoned, in *Analogy of Religion* (1736), that if natural religion (Deism) held similar beliefs to revealed religion, then it was just as reasonable to embrace Christianity. In this context he argued for miracles and the Christian faith as a whole. He hints at his overall method in his conclusion by asserting: "There is no need of abstruse reasonings and distinctions to convince an unprejudiced understanding, that there is a God who made and governs the world, and will judge it in righteousness; . . . For revelation claims to be the voice of God . . . so it offers itself to us with manifest obvious appearances of having something more than human in it, and therefore in all reason requires to have its claims most seriously examined into."[22]

Soon skepticism became the intellectual rage. David Hume (1711–1776) offered a critique of arguments for God's existence and miracles.[23] One of the first to respond was William Paley (1743–1805). His work titled *Natural Theology*, skillfully presented the teleological (from design) argument. His argument unfortunately never received a wide audience because of the controversy surrounding Charles Darwin's *Origin of Species* (1859). Paley authored a second apologetic work, *A View of the Evidences of Christianity*, in which he defended the reliability of the New Testament along with the life, death, and resurrection of Jesus.

Following Hume, Immanuel Kant's (1724–1804) agnosticism gained wide influence, especially his critique of the traditional arguments for God. He attempted to demonstrate that they were dependent on the invalid ontological augment. Many after reading Kant's *Critique of Pure Reason*,[24] felt apologetics could never again begin with arguments for God's existence. Although Kant's agnosticism did not escape critique,[25] many apologists began to express alternative methods for doing apologetics (see chapter 2).

Such skepticism received a response from Scottish Calvinist Thomas Reid (1710–1796). His philosophy, which was later known as

22. Butler, *Analogy of Religion*, 313.

23. See Hume, *Dialogues Concerning Natural Religion* and *Enquiries Concerning Human Understanding and Concerning the Principles of Morals*.

24. Kant, *Critique of Pure Reason*.

25. Flint, *Agnosticism*.

Scottish Common Sense Realism, presented a more complete answer to Hume's skepticism. His work amounted to a revival of Realism that showed how far adrift philosophy had gone. Philosophy, according to Reid, had become so obscure that it could not see what was so obvious to the common person on the street. First Principles, self-evident truths, and right vs. wrong should be obvious because it was the way God created humans.

One prolific and creative Christian author of the 1800s, Søren Kierkegaard (1818–1855), conceptually presented Christian belief with no need to prove its truth claims by argument.[26] His experiential approach rejected all traditional proofs for God and arguments for the deity of Christ. Instead, a blind leap of faith, and an assertion to accept Christian doctrine as paradoxical (e.g., Jesus Christ as God and man is a contradiction), removed any need for rationality. The result was total Fideism.

Two prominent theologians paved the way for apologetics into the twentieth century. Scottish Common Sense Realism influenced both Charles Hodge (1818–1855) and B. B. Warfield (1851–1921). They embraced, if not revived a classical approach to apologetics. Reason, they believed, could be used to discern if Scripture is from God. Once recognized that it was divine in origin, one should submit to its authority. Held to be valid were the traditional arguments for God and historical defense of the Christian faith. Their efforts would also include a defense of Christianity against the doctrinal demise found in theological Liberalism. Liberalism outright rejected the traditional beliefs of Christians. Warfield found Princeton Seminary, as well as many others, to be gradually compromising doctrinal standards due to the influence of Liberalism.

However, important milestones were reached for apologetics as an academic subject during the nineteenth century. Apologetics matured as a scientific subject of study. L. Russ Bush points to K. H. Sack (*Christian Apologetics,* 1829) as "the first to suggest a scientifically organized Christian apologetic."[27] Such a new subject differed widely in approach, methodology, and theological position, but nonetheless established Christian apologetics "as an independent discipline within the field of

---

26. See Kierkegaard, *Concluding Unscientific Postscript to Philosophical Fragments.*
27. Bush, *Classical,* 377.

theological studies, capable of and demanding separate treatment."[28] Another important academic contribution was the recognition that apologetics, as a subject, provided a foundation for the justification and development of systematic theology. Warfield provided an interesting diagram to demonstrate this (Figure 1.1).[29] Near the turn of the twentieth century Warfield had authored an encyclopedic article that clearly defined the subject of apologetics as "the science which establishes the truth of Christianity as the absolute religion."[30]

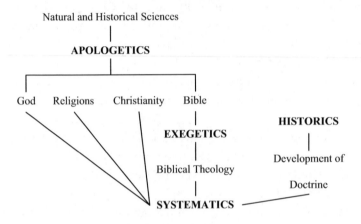

Figure 1.1 Apologetics as the Foundation of Theology

While Warfield and others fought the scholarly battles against Liberalism, little apologetics seemed to trickle down into the Christian pews. One indication of this failure is the effort put forth in 1909 that was funded by two laymen, which resulted in a freely distributed work titled *The Fundamentals*. Originally, in twelve volumes, it was sent to over 300,000 pastors and missionaries. The work employed conservative scholars in various denominations to write in defense of the Christian faith in a number of areas at a level understandable to the pastor and congregation.[31] As Liberalism continued to infect various denominations, a converted Atheist started to introduce apologetics to the populist.

28. Ibid.

29. Warfield, *The Idea of Systematic Theology*, 74.

30. Warfield, "Apologetics."

31. Torrey, et al., *The Fundamentals*.

CONTEMPORARY

During World War II, C. S. Lewis (1898–1963), an Oxford professor, began broadcasting radio messages on apologetic issues in England. Later they were compiled in a book titled *Mere Christianity*. Lewis' creative and literary skills were applied to Christian apologetics and the result was an easily accessible and understandable defense for Christianity. Lewis would go on to write several other books on Christianity and apologetics. He embraced the classical approach of scholars and especially was fond of the moral argument. Lewis remarks how he found such an argument convincing, "My argument against God was that the universe seemed so cruel and unjust. But how had I got this idea of *just* and *unjust?* A man does not call a line crooked unless he has some idea of a straight line."[32]

In an address titled *Christian Apologetics,* made in 1945, Lewis asserted, "One of the great difficulties is to keep before the audience's mind the question of Truth. They always think you are recommending Christianity not because it is *true* but because it is *good.* . . . One must keep on pointing out that Christianity is a statement which, if false, is of *no* importance, and, if true, of infinite importance. The one thing it cannot be is moderately important."[33]

At the same time Lewis was reviving classical apologetics for the populous in England, another scholar in the U. S. was putting a twist on apologetics that was distinctively not classical. Cornelius Van Til (1895–1987) was professor at Westminster Theological Seminary. Van Til fell under the influence of Abraham Kuyper (1837–1920) who reasoned that Christianity cannot be proven to non-Christians. He concluded that all apologetic arguments presupposed Christian principles that non-believers could not accept. Hence, no common ground existed between the Christian and non-Christian.

The Old Princetonian theologians such as Hodge and Warfield also influenced Van Til. He felt that he could combine the two schools by acknowledging some commonality between believer and non-believer such as perception and logic. But he denied any commonality when it came to an appeal to Christian arguments. Arguments, such as the cosmological, were thought invalid when applied to the non-believer

---

32. Lewis, *Mere Christianity*, 45.
33. Lewis, *God in the Dock*, 101.

and at best could only give the believer probability. With such an invalid and incommunicable apologetic, Van Til offered an alternative.
Instead, he developed a method that tried to show that no systems of
thought opposed to Christianity could account for rationality and morality. Then he offered a view starting with the presupposition of the
Christian triune God as the only possible account of reality and life.
In his words, "To argue by presupposition is to indicate what are the
epistemological and metaphysical principles that underlie and control
one's methods. The Reformed apologist will frankly admit that his own
methodology presupposes the truth of Christian theism. Basic to all
doctrines of Christian Theism is that of the self-contained God, or if we
wish, that of the ontological trinity. It is this notion of the ontological
trinity that ultimately controls a truly Christian methodology."[34] Such a
methodology "is therefore based upon presuppositions that are quite the
opposite of those of the non-Christian."[35] His system became known as
Presuppositional Apologetics.

Van Til's system attracted a number of prominent writers that
adapted and changed it to create various spin-offs. Not all would trace
their roots to Van Til, but since the 1950's some that have followed in a
similar vein include Gordon H. Clark, Carl F. H. Henry, Edward John
Carnell, Gordon R. Lewis, Francis Schaeffer, and John M. Frame.[36]

The classical approach continued to attract advocates from the
1950s to the present. Some apologists abandoned the first step of the
classical approach (proving God's existence) to embrace a purely evidential or historical method (e.g., John W. Montgomery).[37] But the classical
approach that came to fruition in the Middle Ages would see a continua-
tion with differing forms and emphasis, in the thought of Stuart Hackett,
Norman Geisler, William Lane Craig, J. P. Moreland, and Catholic Peter
Kreeft. Each of these individuals has authored an academic text in the
subject of apologetics supporting their approach.[38]

34. Van Til, *The Defense of the Faith*, 99–100.

35. Ibid.

36. See Clark, *A Christian View of Men and Things*; Henry, *God, Revelation, and
Authority*; Carnell, *An Introduction to Christian Apologetics*; Lewis, *Testing Christianity's
Truth Claims*; Schaeffer, *The Complete Works of Francis A. Schaeffer*; Frame, *Apologetics
to the Glory Of God*.

37. See Montgomery, *Tractatus Logico-Theologicus*, 115.

38. See Hackett, *The Resurrection of Theism*; Geisler, *Christian Apologetics*; Craig,
Introduction to Apologetics; Moreland, *Scaling the Secular City*; Kreeft and Tacelli, *A

Some more recent trends have attempted to combine various approaches in order to create a more complete system of apologetics that focuses on the individual apologetic needs of the unbeliever. Advocates of this methodology include Ronald Mayers, David Clark, and Kenneth Boa.[39]

This brief sketch of a history of apologetics does not come close to exhausting the individuals or the works that have defended Christianity through the ages (Table 1.1). But what Henry B. Smith, a Christian educator of apologetics eloquently wrote in 1893, still stands today,

> We sometimes think it strange-it almost alarms us-that Christianity should be so desperately assailed; but when we come to think about it, it is the most natural thing in the world. Evil will always attack good; error instinctively assails the truth; sin, by its very nature, is opposite and opposed to holiness. Incarnate Love was crucified between two thieves; and the church cannot expect to be better treated than its head and Lord-it is surely enough for the servant that he be as his Master. Men who cannot find God in nature cannot find God in the Bible. Men who deny the supernatural must consider all religious faith a delusion. Even a heathen might *go on* and find God, but a materialist must *go back*, and deny himself, in order to find him. As long as there are sin and unbelief, so long there will be attacks on Christianity; and there must needs be a defense also.[40]

Hopefully enough has been discussed to demonstrate the continual thread of persons that offered a defense of the Christian faith in the face of all kinds of intellectual opposition.

The task now is to look at contemporary apologetics, its various systems of thought and major advocates, to arrive at a decision concerning an appropriate methodology for a Christian Apologetics Educational program.

Handbook of Christian Apologetics.

39. See Mayers, *Both/And*; Clark, *Dialogical Apologetics*; Boa and Bowman, *Faith has its Reasons*.

40. Smith, *Introduction to Christian Theology Apologetics*, 118–119.

Period of Formulation:	New Testament & Church Fathers	Middle Ages	Modern		Contemporary	
Period of Development:	A.D. 30–400	400–1400	1400–1900		1900–Present	
System or Classification:	Reactionary	Classical	Experiential	Evidential/Historical	Presuppositional	Combinational
Proponent:	Origen (ca. 185–254)	Aquinas (1224/5–1274)	Søren Kierkegaard (1818–1855)	Joseph Butler (1692–1752)	Cornelius Van Til (1895–1987)	Various
Description:	Responds to religious objections, problems, or misunderstandings concerning the Christian faith.	Uses rational arguments to demonstrate God's existence, nature, and evidence for the historical truth of Christianity.	Shifts away from arguments for God to a blind faith acceptance of Christianity.	Emphasis on historical or other evidences for Christianity.	Reliance on the presuppositions of Christian revelation (e.g., Triune God).	Combines various apologetic systems and uses them, as needed, to argue for Christianity.

Table 1.1 Apologetic Systems through History

QUESTIONS TO ANSWER

1. Give a biblical definition of apologetics and discuss how it has become a subject of study today?

2. Explain how each period of history dealt with the question of God's existence and evidence for Christianity.

3. If you had to choose the most significant period in the history of apologetics, what would it be and why.

SELECT READINGS

Avery Dulles, *A History of Apologetics.*

Kenneth D. Boa and Robert M. Bowman, Jr. *Faith has its Reasons.* Chapter1.

Fredrick R. Howe, *Challenge and Response.* Chapter 1.

2

Apologetic Systems

OBJECTIVES

Explain how each system of apologists is different in its approach.

Discern the value of classical apologetics as it relates to education.

A POLOGISTS HAVE FOR THE most part agreed *that* the faith should be defended but they have not all agreed on *how* the faith should be defended. Various Apologetic methods have emerged over the years. As we saw in the last chapter, it started with an early reactionary approach evident in the writings of Church Fathers to a splintering of clearly distinct and sometimes opposing methodologies. To complicate matters further, there is little agreement today upon the use of terminology to help classify apologetic systems. While there is some overlap and agreement among some apologetic systems, the overall emphasis and philosophy is usually evident in the following four classifications: Classical, Evidential, Experiential, and Presuppositional.[1] The Christian secondary school is also not immune to the influence of different methods or systems of doing apologetics. While most schools are able to classify their method of apologetics, as many as 18 percent cannot identify their apologetic method. In what follows, each classification is explained and some major objections raised concerning the classical system are answered. This is done to clarify and argue for a proper methodology to be used in a CAE program of study.

1. Norman L. Geisler, "Apologetics, Types of" in *Baker Encyclopedia of Christian Apologetics* (Grand Rapids: Baker, 1999), 41–44.

CLASSICAL

Although according to our survey (see Appendix A) only 7 percent of secondary Christian schools describe their apologetic method as classical, it is incipiently rooted in the New Testament. The Apostle Paul acknowledged that there was common intellectual ground with non-believers for the existence of God (Rom 1:21) and that evidence concerning the resurrection of Jesus Christ could be used to convince others (1 Cor 15:1–8). These two basic steps have come to define the classical approach to apologetics. Early Christians, following the apostle's method, rarely found need in a theistic and polytheistic culture to defend the existence of God. Instead, they found themselves using apologetics on a reactionary basis against false teachings and defending various aspects of the gospel when needed. The full classical approach did not find intellectual and systematic expression until the Middle Ages.

The classical approach is characterized by stressing rational[2] arguments for the existence of God. This is viewed as a necessary first step to be combined or followed with a second step that presents evidence to support the claim that Christianity is historically true. The first step accepts that at least some version of the three traditional arguments, known as the cosmological, teleological, and axiological, for God's existence are true in an undeniable sense. This does not mean that some do not deny the arguments, only that they are logically valid and that each premise naturally leads to the conclusion that God exists. Most reject a fourth type of argument, known as the Ontological, but some do see value in a definitional understanding of God that can be combined with other arguments. The second step presents historical evidence concerning the New Testament's reliability, its claim of deity for Jesus, and his resurrection from the dead.

The major Medieval proponents of this approach include Augustine, (354–430 AD), Anselm (1033–1109 AD), and Thomas Aquinas (1224/5–1274 AD). Significant modern advocates include John Locke, William Paley, C. H. Hodge, and B. B. Warfield. Contemporary supporters include C. S. Lewis, Stuart Hackett, Norman Geisler, William Lane Craig, J. P. Moreland, Peter Kreeft, and Winfried Corduan.[3]

2. While it can be characterized as *rational* most advocates would reject the label *rationalistic* which carries the understanding that everything can be known, determined, or explained by human reason such as that found in the philosophy of René Descartes.

3. C. S. Lewis, *Mere Christianity* (New York: Macmillan, 1952); Stuart Hackett,

EVIDENTIAL

Only 6 percent of secondary Christian schools describe their apologetics program as exclusively evidential. This approach stresses evidence that may be rational, historical, archaeological, experiential, etc. Such emphasis is usually done to the neglect, rejection, or misplacement of rational arguments for the existence of God. Some advocates may rely to a certain extent on arguments for God, but they are usually considered to be probabilistic, helpful, or not needed to establishing a theistic structure for understanding the Christian claims. Evidentialist John Warwick Montgomery pointedly states, "one does not need such a structure [theistic] to understand what Jesus meant in claiming divinity for himself or to appreciate the force of the argument for the significance of his resurrection."[4] In contrast, a classical approach not only insists on the theistic world view, but states such arguments for God are undeniably true. Most evidentialists are concerned with combining evidence and building a culminating case for Christianity; similar to an attorney in a courtroom. Some may have a specific focus exclusively in a certain area such as historical or scientific evidence. The conviction of the evidentialist methodology is that such evidence is so strong, in its amount or in strength; it can convince a non-believer (even in a non-theistic world view) that Christianity (including God's existence) is true.

Some ancient advocates in early Christianity that seemed to embrace this methodology included Justin Martyr and Origen. A modern proponent is William Paley. Some contemporary authors using this method include Bernard Ramm, John Warwick Montgomery, Josh McDowell, and Gary Habermas.[5]

The Resurrection of Theism (Grand Rapids, Baker, 1957), Norman L. Geisler, *Christian Apologetics* (Grand Rapids: Baker, 1976), William Lane Craig, *Introduction to Apologetics* (Chicago: Moody Press, 1984), J. P. Moreland, *Scaling the Secular City* (Grand Rapids: Baker, 1987), Peter Kreeft and Ronald K. Tacelli, *A Handbook of Christian Apologetics* (Colorado Springs: NavPress, 1997); Winfried Corduan, *Reasonable Faith: Basic Christian Apologetics* (Nashville: Broadman & Holman, 1993).

4. John Warwick Montgomery, *Tractatus Logico-Theologicus* (Bonn, Germany: Kultur und Wissenschaft, 2002), 115.

5. Bernard Ramm, *Protestant Christian Evidences: A Textbook of the Evidences of the Truthfulness of the Christian faith for Conservative Protestants* (Chicago: Moody Press, 1953); John Warwick Montgomery, *History and Christianity: A Vigorous, Convincing Presentation of the Evidences for a Historical Jesus* (Minneapolis: Bethany, 1965); Josh McDowell, *Evidence That Demands A Verdict* (San Bernardino: Here's Life, 1972); Gary R. Habermas, *The Resurrection of Jesus* (Grand Rapids: Baker, 1980).

EXPERIENTIAL

An experiential approach at first may seem to be a sub-classification under evidentialist. But a few points of emphasis distinguish this approach as a distinct classification. For one, only the subjective Christian experience is used for evidence. Other forms of evidence or rational argumentation for God's existence are rejected for various reasons. Two types of experience are usually offered. First, the general culminating experience that humanity has had with God is available to all and offered to encourage personal belief in God. Second, a special personal experience that may be characterized as mystical, supernatural, or an existential leap of faith is emphasized. Experience itself is the authenticating claim for Christianity, even though some proponents may not even believe this is necessary. The more extreme advocates would espouse Fideism. This is the belief that there is no reason to be given for faith. The faith experience itself is not viewed as a reason for faith. It is understood as a self-authenticating, non-rational, and direct encounter with God that is more real than any other experience.

Modern and contemporary advocates of a specific or individual experience are Meister Eckart, Søren Kierkegaard, Rudolph Bultmann, and Karl Barth. Those emphasizing the general experience of humanity include Friedrich Schleiermacher and Paul Tillich.[6]

PRESUPPOSITIONAL

While only 6 percent of secondary Christian schools are self described as presupposition, there are several different versions of presuppositionalism (Table 2.1). It seems however, that they all hold to some extent that Christianity must be defended based on certain presuppositions or axioms that are either based on the assumption of Christian revelation or ground that is considered unprovable (at least to the non-believer). A presupposition supposes the basic truth of Christianity and then tries to show in various ways that Christianity alone is true. Most presuppositionalist reject rational arguments for the existence of God. Some

6. Søren Kierkegaard, *Concluding Unscientific Postscript to Philosophical Fragments*, vol. 1, trans. Howard V. and Edna H. Hong (Princeton: Princeton University Press, 1985); Rudolf Bultmann, *What is Theology?* trans. Roy A. Harrisville (Minneapolis: Fortress Press, 1997; Friedrich Schleiermacher, *On Religion: Speeches to Its Cultured Despisers* (Louisville: Westminster, 1994); Paul Tillich, *Dynamics of Faith* (New York: Harper, 1957).

may view them as only probabilistic instead of undeniable. Some accept the supposed devastating critique that Immanuel Kant leveled against the traditional arguments in his *Critique of Pure Reason*.[7] Five versions of presuppositionalism are considered here: Revelational, Rational, Systematic Consistency, Practical and Reformed Epistemology. A sixth version, Combinational, will be treated as a new emerging system of apologetics but could also be placed under one or more of the above categories for reasons we suggest below.

Revelational

Revelational presuppositionalism posits the triune God (Trinity), as revealed in Scripture, as the only basis for truth, meaning, logic, value, etc. In this approach, these things can be known and used only because we have been created by God with the capacity to know Him. Cornelius Van Til's argument by presupposition contains two steps. The first step is to show that all non-Christian systems of thought are unable to account for rationality and morality. This is nothing short of showing that all non-Christian systems are irrational. The second step is to present the Christian world view as the only possible presupposition for thinking and living. This method is primarily a transcendental argument that uses the law of non-contradictions (that 'A' is not 'non-A') as a test. Van Til summarized his view as "the only absolute certain proof of the truth of Christianity is that unless its truth be presupposed there is no proof of anything. Christianity is proved as being the very foundation of the idea of proof itself."[8] Proponents, with different versions of this approach are Van Til and John Frame.[9]

Rational

Rational presuppositionalism maintains that only what is given through biblical revelation can truly be known. The Bible is understood as an axiom, something assumed without proof. Hence, there is nothing to prove about the Bible, there are only truths to deduce from Scripture.

7. Immanuel Kant, *Critique of Pure Reason,* trans. Werner S. Pluhar (Indianapolis: Hackett, 1996). Perhaps the best rebuttal to this influence in apologetics is found in Stuart Hackett's *The Resurrection of Theism.*

8. Cornelius Van Til, *The Defense of the Faith* (Phillipsburg: P & R, 1967), 298.

9. John M. Frame, *Apologetics to the Glory of God: An Introduction* (Phillipsburg: P & R, 1994).

This apologetic consists of two steps. The first is to show that non-Christian philosophies are internally inconsistent. The second step is to demonstrate that Christianity is internally consistent. The method is deductive reasoning and the test is internal consistency. Advocates of this version include Gordon Clark and Carl F. H. Henry.[10]

Systematic Consistency

Systematic consistency presuppositionalism defends Christianity by comprehensively taking into account all relevant evidences. If Christianity is found to be internally consistent philosophically and externally consistent with historical and scientific facts, then it is true. Edward John Carnell, explains "Christianity is true because its major elements are consistent with one another and with the broad facts of history and nature"[11] What makes this view Presuppositional is that God's existence, or the triune God, is understood as an assumption or axiom. Edward John Carnell and Gordon Lewis have different versions of this approach.[12]

Practical

Practical presuppositionalism defends Christianity by concentrating on the evidence that shows non-Christian systems to be unlivable with their presuppositions and that only Christianity is livable with its presuppositions. Hence, false systems are unlivable, and only Christianity is consistently livable and therefore believable. There may also be an emphasis on individualizing an apologetics approach and on showing the non-Christian's existential need. Francis Schaeffer has championed this view and commented: "*The truth that we let in first is not a dogmatic statement of the truth of the Scriptures, but the truth of the external world and the truth of what man himself is.* This is what shows him his need. The Scriptures then show him the real nature of his lostness and the answer to

10. Gordon H. Clark, *In Defense of Theology* (Milford: Mott Media, 1984); Carl F. H. Henry, *God Revelation, and Authority* (Waco: Word, 1976–1983).

11. Edward J. Carnell, *Christian Commitment: An Apologetic* (Grand Rapids: Baker, 1982), 286.

12. Gordon R. Lewis, *Testing Christianity's Truth Claims: Approaches to Christian Apologetics* (New York: University Press of America, 1990); Edward J. Carnell, *An Introduction to Christian Apologetics* (Grand Rapids: Eerdmans, 1948).

it. *This, I am convinced, is the truth order of our apologetics in the second half of the twentieth century for people living under the line of despair.*"[13]

Reformed Epistemology

About 3 percent of secondary Christian schools acknowledge themselves as Reformed Epistemology. This version of presuppositionalism finds its roots in the thinking of Christian philosopher Alvin Plantinga. Plantinga has never published a text on Christian apologetics, but he has written a justification for Christian belief.[14] His epistemological understanding of belief in God, has found favor with a number of apologists. While not limited to them, this is particularly true of the reformed position. It is grounded in an epistemological understanding that rejects the need to rationally argue for God's existence. Plantinga critiques classical foundationalism, which he understands to be the tradition of Thomas Aquinas that supposedly says one is rational only when their belief is either immediately basic or reducible to something basic such as an undeniable first principle or self-evident proposition.[15] Plantinga argues that the truth of this foundationalism is neither reducible to a first principle nor is it a basic belief. Hence, it is unable to stand on its own criterion and is self-referentially inconsistent. Plantinga then suggests that belief in God is, as he puts it, "properly basic" needing no more justification than anything else that is immediately known to a person. That is, belief in God is not the result of reasonable proofs or evidences. Plantinga argues that, "The believer doesn't need natural theology in order to achieve rationality or epistemic propriety in believing; his belief in God can be perfectly rational even if he knows of no cogent argument, deductive or inductive, for the existence of God-indeed, even if there *isn't* any such argument."[16] Hence, he rejects any necessity of natural theology. It is interesting that

---

13. Francis A. Schaeffer, *The Complete Works of Francis A. Schaeffer: A Christian Worldview*, vol. 1 A Christian View of Philosophy and Culture, 2d ed. (Wheaton: Crossway Books, 1982), 140–41.

14. See Alvin Plantinga and Nicholas Wolterstorff, eds., *Faith and Rationality: Reason and Belief in God* (Notre Dame: University of Notre Dame Press, 1983) and Alvin Plantinga, *Warranted Christian Belief* (New York: Oxford University Press, 2000).

15. A basic belief is something known or evident to the individual such as "I ate breakfast this morning" or "there is a glass of water on the table."

16. Alvin Plantinga, "Reason and Belief in God," in *The Analytical Theist*, ed. James F. Sennett (Grand Rapids: Eerdmans, 1988), 140.

some who accept his critique of foundationalism still hold to some value or usefulness for rational arguments.[17]

Presuppositionalism Compared					
Type	Revelational	Rational	Systematic Consistency	Practical	Reformed Epistemology
Presupposition	Trinity	Bible	Christian World view	Christian World view	Proper Basicality
Test	Non–contradiction	Internal Coherence	Internal & External Coherence	Livability	Other justified true beliefs.
Proponent	C. Van Til	G. Clark	E. J. Carnell	F. Schaeffer	A. Plantinga

Table 2.1 Presuppositionalism Compared

COMBINATIONAL

Another recent approach to apologetics seems to have taken over the apologetics method in secondary Christian schools. Thirty-eight percent describe themselves as combinational. This method combines what is believed to be all the strengths of the previous methods together. From a modern standpoint almost all the methods of apologetics are combinational. Even the classical method sees the necessity of combining rational arguments that demonstrate the existence of God with historical arguments for Christianity. But combinationalism sees value in all the apologetic methods, but does not accept any of the previously mentioned methods as being an adequate or complete system of apologetics. Hence, it combines what is believed to be the best from each system and offers it as a more adequate apologetic.[18] For example, a combinational

17. Two recent works that value Plantinga's critique of foundationalism but then go on to express some helpfulness of arguments for God include one popular book by John G. Stackhouse, Jr. *Humble Apologetics: Defending the Faith Today* (Oxford: Oxford University Press, 2002 and a college text book by James E. Taylor, *Introducing Apologetic: Cultivating Christian Commitment* (Grand Rapids: Baker Academic, 2006), 29–37. See my review of both books "Humble Apologetics: Defending the Faith Today." Book Review in *Christian Apologetics Journal*. 4, no. 2, (2005): 100–103 and "Introducing Apologetics: Cultivating Christian Commitment." Book Review in *Christian Apologetics Journal*. 8, no. 2, (2009).

18. Despite warnings and cautions to not "be interpreted as proposing a 'new approach' or a comprehensive system . . ." it nonetheless seems to do this. Kenneth Boa and Robert Bowman. *Faith has its Reasons: An Integrated Approach to Defending Christianity* (Colorado Springs, CO: NavPress, 2001), 535.

approach may use the unliveability of other world views emphasized by practical presuppositionalism and then use arguments for God's existence as a helpful guide to discovering what is true about a world view. This combinational method usually emphasizes a personalized or 'dialogical' approach to apologetics, offering the individual only what he or she needs to believe that Christianity is true. It tries to identify and include cultural, ethnic, and social needs of the individual in order to tailor an apologetic towards that specific individual.

Modern proponents of this view include Ronald Mayers, David Clark, and Kenneth Boa.[19] Historically some combinationalists trace their roots back to E. J. Carnell.

A DEFENSE OF THE CLASSICAL APPROACH

While it is beyond the scope of this book to present a complete case for classical apologetics, there are some important objections to answer and especially reasons to embrace this approach for educational purposes.

Invalid or Misplaced Arguments For God

There are two main objections raised by the non-classical methodologies. One is that traditional proofs for the existence of God are invalid. The second includes the placement (or location) of arguments for God's existence in the overall apologetic.

Opposing methods have followed knowingly or unknowingly in the skeptical footsteps of Immanuel Kant and others. But the classical approach to apologetics has not been shown invalid by such skeptics. Opposing methods have critiqued the classical approach for not having any universally recognizable common ground on which to build an argument for God.[20] This however, ignores or misunderstands the nature of first principles that are grounded in being or existence. For example, the statement "something exists" is existentially undeniable since it is self-defeating to deny one's existence. Once understood the first principle is intuitively realized universally and is a claim about reality. As one philosopher reminds us, "[first] principles do not provide any

---

19. Ronald B. Mayers, *Both/And: A Balanced Apologetic* (Chicago: Moody Press, 1984); David K. Clark, *Dialogical Apologetics* (Grand Rapids: Baker, 1993); Boa, *Faith has its Reasons*.

20. Boa, *Faith has its Reasons*, 150, cf. 151.

real knowledge unless they first apply to the data of sense experience."[21] Hence, it is not dependent upon one's world view. This is not to suggest that one could not doubt the principle, but only that one could not argue to the contrary of the principle since it is an indemonstrable truth to which demonstrations may be reduced. It is not a starting point in the mind alone (*a priori*). A statement corresponds to reality; as such, it has undeniable existence. Such a starting point should be distinguished from the starting point known as the principle of sufficient reason which would place the principle purely in the realm of reason. Basing the argument on the existential undeniability demands a ground in reality. This is a crucial point since most forms of the cosmological argument follow Descartes who grounds the argument in the *a priori* or reason alone. Critiques of such arguments do not apply to valid cosmological arguments based on existential undeniability. Hence, if the starting point is universal and undeniable than a valid argument for God's existence based on it will also be true in an undeniable sense.[22]

Furthermore, the affirmation that "there are no universally accepted principles that are true" is either self-defeating or just wrong. If the statement is put forth as a universal truth then, either that statement is a universally accepted true principle itself, in which case it denies itself, or it is not a universally accepted true principle in which case it has no basis for universal acceptance. Similarly, a statement of denial regarding such universal principles may not be self-defeating, but since we have identified the existence of such a principle, it is simply wrong.

As mentioned earlier Alvin Plantinga's objection to rational arguments for God's existence has found fertile ground among apologists. However, there are significant problems with his analysis and critique.[23]

21. Etienne Gilson, "Can the Existence of God Still be Demonstrated?" in *The McAuley Lectures, 1960 Saint Thomas Aquinas and Philosophy* (West Harford: Saint Joseph College, 1960), 7.

22. For an example of such an argument see Norman L. Geisler, *Christian Apologetics* (Grand Rapids, Baker Books, 1976), 237–59 or Norman Geisler and Winfried Corduan, *Philosophy of Religion*, 2d ed. (Grand Rapids, Baker Books, 1988), 175–207. For the use of this type of argumentation in a modern debate see Terry Miethe and Antony Flew, *Does God Exist: A Believer and an Atheist Debate* (New York: HarperSanFrancisco, 1991).

23. See the insightful critique offered by Barney H. Corbin, "A Thomistic Reply to the Reformed Objection to Natural Theology" *Christian Apologetics Journal* 5 no. 2 (2006) : 65–107 and Leonard A. Kennedy, ed. *Thomistic Papers IV* (Houston: The Center for Thomistic Studies, 1988).

First, it is doubtful that the strict foundationalism Plantinga attributes to Aquinas is actually attributable to him. Aquinas acknowledges other ways people can legitimately come to believe in God and even admits that few may have the time or ability to argue for God's existence. Yet, at the same time, this does not negate the validness of human reason and argument being used to conclude that God does exist. To deny this is to suggest the absurd conclusion that humans do not need to be rational. Second, the existence of God is not properly basic in the same way as a self-evident proposition or other things immediately known to us. As Barney Corbin clarifies, "In natural theology Thomas is using human reason and observation to find out what kinds of things can be known about; not just reality but ultimate reality as well. This leads Thomas to look for the Ultimate Cause of all things (i.e., God) as He is related to His creation. Thus the existence of God can be known 'through,' or 'by' His effects in nature making natural theology a legitimate science. . . ."[24] So, as others have said, we cannot assert that God's existence is just basic for the same reason that we cannot assert that the Great Pumpkin's existence is properly basic.[25] Furthermore, it is worth noting that Aquinas is working from a metaphysical realism in which things exist independent of our thinking (i.e., there is a real external knowable world) while Plantinga seems to be working from the Kantian philosophy that assumes a gulf between an unknowable world and a mind that structures what is knowable. This is hardly a solid philosophical ground upon which to rest an educational approach to apologetics.

Concerning the placement of arguments for God's existence, the evidentialist insists that it is not necessary to establish a theistic framework prior to "understand what Jesus meant in claiming divinity for himself."[26] Jesus himself, it is argued, when asked, "Show us the Father," simply said, "He who has seen me, has seen the Father."[27] What is missed by the evidentialist is that Jesus was already speaking in a Theistic context (i.e., Judaism) to individuals that already had a proper concept of only one Deity (as opposed to an Eastern teaching of one among many other deities). So it was not necessary for Jesus, or any other apologist, to establish a theistic world view if one already exists. On the other hand

24. Corbin, "A Thomistic Reply," 80–81.

25. Ibid., 91.

26. Montgomery, *Tractatus*, 115.

27. Ibid.

when an apologist finds himself in a non-theistic setting the first step of classical apologetics is necessary or the risk of truth not being understood may prevail. Paul, as an example in Acts 17, faced such a situation and started his apologetic by establishing who the true God is, before explaining the Deity and resurrection of Jesus.

Invalidity of Historical Arguments

There are at least two main objections leveled by some non-classical methods at the second step of classical apologetics. The first concerns the nature of historical facts and the second is the objectivity of historical investigation.

Historical evidence concerns facts. But it is argued that facts in themselves are never neutral, raw, or self-interpreting. They are always understood in the context of a person's world view. Hence, such facts have no evidential value for someone who does not hold to a Christian perspective (i.e., world view). It is true that a world view is always prior and necessary to the interpretation of historical facts. For example, if someone proves Jesus' resurrection historically (a fact), it is not logically necessary to conclude that the Christian God raised Jesus from the dead. A Hindu (polytheist) might conclude that he is one god among several or a secular humanist (atheist) might call the event an anomaly that is yet to be explained in natural terms. Neither position is forced to conclude by the fact of the resurrection alone that there is a God. But only the historical evidentialist is confronted with this objection. The classical approach to Christian apologetics provides a solution to this objection by performing its first step of arguing for a theistic world view.

Another historical concern involves the claim that objectivity in historical investigation is impossible. Historians, it is argued, always have a bias or an agenda that skews their interpretation of history. Hence, any historical apologetic will have a bias that comes through when offering historical evidence for the Christian faith. This objection again fails to note the value of the first step; proving a theistic world view. Historical objectivity is achievable and provable in a theistic world view. Furthermore, universal claims to the contrary such as "all historians are biased" or "no historians are unbiased" do not negate objectivity. Instead they call into question what is a proper method of inquiry (i.e., historiography). A proper method must be used to yield results that fit the true world view. Hence, the historian's world view is essential to the context of a proper methodology. The nature of historical inquiry calls for a historical analysis to yield, at best, highly probable results. Philosopher Jacques Maritain (1882–1973) maintains that, "for the historian it is a prerequisite that he have a sound philosophy of man, an integrated culture, an accurate appreciation of the human being's various activities and their comparative importance, a correct scale of moral, political, religious, technical and artistic values. The value, I mean the truth, of the historical work will be in proportion to the human richness of the historian."[28] Maritain continues, "Such a position implies no subjectivism. There is truth in history. . . . But the truth of history is factual, not rational truth; it can therefore be substantiated only through signs— after the fashion in which any individual and existential datum is to be checked; and thought in many respects it can be known not only in a conjectural manner but with certainty."[29]

Experience Alone Can Establish Christian Faith

Certainly, one's personal conversion experience is important. However, experience itself is neither true nor false and can have no definitive function in discovering the absolute truth of a religion. There are no self-evident religious experiences. Professor Norman Geisler pointedly states, "Truth is found in expression about the object of our experiences, not in the experiences themselves."[30] There is also no religious experience that is self interpreting or transferable. As Geisler notes, making such an assertion confuses the source of truth (i.e., God) with the support for truth (i.e., rational argument and evidence). Such reasoning offered in the context of proving Christianity begs the question. In other words, experience can be a source of truth about God, but not a test for truth. Furthermore, Fideism, the belief that there are no reasons to become a Christian, is simply self-defeating since the belief itself is offered as a reasoned approach to Christianity.

No System of Apologetics is Sufficient

The combinational approach to apologetics may at first seem helpful in dealing with different methodologies. But upon closer examination it

28. Jacques Maritain, *On the Philosophy of History* (Clifton, NJ: Kelley, 1973), 7–8.

29. Ibid., 8.

30. Geisler, "Experiential Apologetics" in *Baker Encyclopedia*, 237.

suffers the same fate as other non-classical approaches. The combinationalist must answer the question of how combining insufficient (or incomplete) systems will result in a sufficient (or more complete) system. It is more complex then just trying to construct a working engine from non-working engine parts. The question is: Can someone build a working engine out of six differently manufactured engines that do not work? This is not possible of course unless the apologist acknowledges one system as true in an area that distinguishes it from the others. If that is the case, however, then the combinationalist ceases to be a pure combinationalist or assumes the use of one method under the identity of another. For example, to admit that the classical arguments for God's existence are true and then combine them with a presuppositional critique, results in just being a classical apologist by a different name who may have confused his case for Christianity. Likewise, if the combinationalist rejects the classical arguments for God, then he is just an evidentialist or presuppositionalist by a different name. Hence, one is forced to be convinced that a system is true, or reject apologetic systems all together thus forsaking a biblical imperative (1 Pet 3:15). Hence, the intention of the combinationalist to build a better apologetic may be admirable, but the results are unsuccessful.

EDUCATIONAL REASONS FOR CLASSICAL APOLOGETICS

There are several reasons to embrace a classical approach to apologetics for the sake of educational integrity. First, classical apologetics is the apologetic system embraced by many orthodox teachers throughout the history of the church (see page 36 Table 2.2). From the time of the Apostle Paul to today, there is a current stream of thought that has expressed and relied on the classical approach (see Chapter 1). Paul used reason to acknowledge the evidence in nature for God's existence (Rom 1:18–21). Hints of the classical approach can be found in some early Church Fathers. Medieval theologians, such as Augustine and Aquinas, used the approach. Protestant, such as Calvin, Paley, Hodge, and Warfield acknowledged or used the classical approach. Likewise, there are many resent scholars that embraced this approach.

Second, there is a reason for the long history and use of the classical approach. It is logically necessary to argue for God's existence prior to arguing for any historical truth of Christianity. If there is no God, how can there be a word of God or a Son of God? This is an important point to consider for educational purposes. Students will sense an intellectual void if demonstrating God's existence is not covered or not in the proper placement (order of demonstration) in an apologetic curriculum. Furthermore, if it is not presented in a manner that shows the truth (i.e., undeniability) of such argument, then it will undermine all other areas of apologetic work. A logically prior vacuum will always exist in the student's thinking that will ultimately collapse any later apologetic reasoning. While some forms of the traditional argument for God's existence have been critiqued and shown to be invalid, there does remain a valid expression in the classical tradition that can be embraced.[31]

Third, the apologetic systems opposed to the classical approach have significant biblical and theological problems. An individual cannot possibly fulfill the biblical imperative of contending for the complete Faith (Jude 3), if God's existence is left out of the equation. If common ground does exist, then it is the biblical responsibility of the believer to provide an answer (1 Pet 3:15). Only the classical approach adequately achieves this. Furthermore, other systems confuse the delicate arena of faith and reason. Classical apologetics concerns giving reasons *that* Christianity is true. It is never to prove faith *in* God or Christ. There can be reasons for faith or a reasonable faith, but the personal acceptance is left to the work and power of the Holy Spirit.[32] Other approaches are unable to keep this balance. Experientialism eliminates reason altogether. Presuppositionalism and Evidentialism simply cut off access to reasoning *that* God exists. A combinational approach reduces to one of the other approaches if the first step of proving God's existence is not necessary or true.

Fourth, a practical problem emerges when a non-classical approach is introduced regarding questions about God. What is the student to do in the face of such difficult questions about the nature of God, evil, or miracles? A presuppositional and evidential approach is left with no justified context or world view to understand a theistic answer. This is hardly the approach of apologetics that helps the educational enterprise. Practically we are left with an ill-equipped and incomplete answer or no answer at all.

---

31. Norman L. Geisler, *Christian Apologetics* (Grand Rapids: Baker, 1976), 237–59.

32. For an excellent explanation of this point see Norman L. Geisler, *Thomas Aquinas: An Evangelical Appraisal* (Grand Rapids: Baker, 1991), 57–69.

Fifth, the classical approach can incorporate what is deemed by some to be valuable in other systems of apologetics. If the approach does not oppose what distinguishes the classical system then it can be incorporated without compromising the approach. For example, there is nothing that opposes the classical approach in pointing out the un-livablity of non-Christian world views. There is no problem presenting experiential evidence either. The problem arises when one forsakes the defining nature of the classical approach (e.g., rational arguments for God's existence) and exclusively relies on non-classical systems for an apologetic. Additionally, there is nothing in the classical approach that prohibits personal sensitivity to ethnic, cultural, and social settings. Individual assessments will always make an apologetic more meaningful to the individual. Such arguments should center on answering and meeting the students immediate needs, yet such effort should not compromise a complete argument that contends for the faith (Jude 3). An approach to apologetics that is classical can, and for educational reasons, should incorporate these aspects.

The problems with non-classical approaches to apologetics do not serve the Christian educational enterprise. It fails on biblical, logical, and experiential grounds. Only the classical approach upholds and respects biblical imperatives, human intellect, and experience. This being the case, we are on solid ground for building an educational philosophy that will incorporate a classical approach to apologetics.

HISTORY AND THE CLASSIFICATION OF APOLOGETICS

The following chart, while not intended to be comprehensive, summarizes some important historical persons (Chapter 1) in apologetics and identifies their system of apologetics (Chapter 2).

Historical Period/Person		Apologetic System/Classification
I.	**The New Testament**	
	A. Verses on Apologetics	Imperative Commands
	B. Apostle Paul	Incipient Classical
II.	**Early Church Fathers**	
	A. Justin Martyr (ca. 100–165)	Reactionary
	B. Origen (ca. 185–254)	Reactionary
III.	**Middle Ages**	
	A. Augustine (354–430)	Classical
	B. Anselm (1033–1109)	Classical
	C. Aquinas (1224/5–1274)	Classical
	D. Meister Eckhart (ca.1260 – 1327/8)	Experiential
IV.	**Reformation**	
	A. Philip Melanchthon (1497–1560)	Classical
	B. John Calvin (1509–1564)	Classical (Implicitly)
V.	**Modern**	
	A. Hugo Grotus (1583–1645)	Classical
	B. Blaise Pascal (1623–1662)	Evidential
	C. Joseph Butler's (1692–1752)	Evidential
	D. William Paley (1743–1805)	Classical
	E. Thomas Reid (1710–1796)	Rationalistic
	F. Friedrich Schleiermacher (1768–1834)	Experiential (General)
	G. Søren Kierkegaard (1818–1855)	Experiential (Fideistic)
	H. Charles Hodge (1851–1878)	Classical
	I. B. B. Warfield (1851–1921)	Classical
VI.	**Contemporary**	
	A. C. S. Lewis (1898–1963)	Classical
	B. Cornelius Van Til (1895–1987)	Presuppositional (Revelational)
	C. Paul Tillich (1886–1965)	Experiential (General)
	D. Rudolph Bultmann (1884–1976)	Experiential (Individual)
	E. Karl Barth (1886–1968)	Experiential (Individual)
	F. Edward John Carnell (1919–1967)	Presuppositional (Consistency)
	G. Gordon H. Clark (1902–1985)	Presuppositional (Rational)
	H. Carl F. H. Henry (1913–2003)	Presuppositional (Rational)
	I. Francis Schaeffer (1912–1984)	Presuppositional (Practical)
	J. Bernard Ramm (1916–1992)	Evidential
	K. Gordon R. Lewis	Presuppositional (Consistency)
	L. Stuart Hackett	Classical (Rationalistic)
	M. Clark Pinnock	Evidential
	N. John Warwick Montgomery	Evidential
	O. R. C. Sproul	Classical
	P. Josh McDowell	Evidential (Historical)
	Q. Norman L. Geisler	Classical
	R. William Lane Craig	Classical
	S. J. P. Moreland	Classical
	T. John M. Frame	Presuppositional (Revelational)
	U. Peter Kreeft	Classical (Roman Catholic)
	V. Ronald Mayers	Combinational
	W. Winfred Corduan	Classical
	X. David Clark	Combinational
	Y. Kenneth Boa	Combinational

Table 2.2 Persons and Apologetic Systems

QUESTIONS TO ANSWER

1. Contrast each system of apologetics.

2. What advantages does the classical method have over the other systems of apologetics?

3. Select an apologetics system and discuss its strengths and weaknesses in relation to teaching students apologetics.

SELECT READINGS

Norman L. Geisler, *Christian Apologetics.* Chapter 1–8.

Kenneth D. Boa and Robert M. Bowman, Jr. *Faith has its Reasons.* Part 2–6.

Frederic R. Howe, *Challenge and Response.* Chapter 9.

3

The Case for Christian Apologetics Education in the Secondary School

OBJECTIVES

Evaluate our contemporary culture to discover the need for apologetics.

Explain how the secondary school student is suited to handle the subject of apologetics.

APOLOGETICS IS A LEGITIMATE subject of study for Christian educational purposes. The basis of this is grounded biblically as well as historically (Chapters 1 and 2). Yet, this alone does not justify the subject's inclusion in a Christian philosophy of education at the secondary level. In this chapter, we justify apologetics as a subject of study to be included in a secondary curriculum. To do this we will first discuss the need that exists for apologetics as a subject of study in our contemporary world. Second, we will justify its inclusion by discussing the educational value and appropriateness the subject has for the student at the secondary level. Finally, we will answer some common objections the educator of apologetics might face when trying to implement the subject.

A CONTEMPORARY NEED

Many societal indicators suggest a strong need for educators to incorporate apologetics into a Christian education curriculum. We are living in a world that is increasingly antagonistic towards the Christian faith. Truth is considered relative and religion is reduced to an individual preference. Few believers, perhaps to no fault of their own, have ever taken a class or read a book on Christian apologetics. Many churches and Christian educational programs have reaped the consequences of such neglect. Young people, at an alarming rate, are going off to college and entering the workforce having abandoned their evangelical faith. In 1995, 10 percent of teens considered themselves evangelical. In 1999 the number had dropped to just 4 percent.[1] This number is closely paralleled by a similar decline among evangelical adults. The evangelical community is falling into deceptive practices and beliefs because of rejecting this valuable foundation to theological studies. The challenging questions of skeptical, and sometimes cynical, professors and unbelieving friends are too difficult for untrained Christians to handle. Many youth, even in Christian churches, hold decidedly non-Christian beliefs. The statistics among youth today support this observation.[2] Many continue to be unaware of the evidence for the Christian faith. Often they will choose to abandon belief for some other religion, philosophy, or cult that makes them feel good or accepted. A presentation of some of the major threats to young, as well as seasoned Christians will emphasize the importance of equipping them to understand, articulate, and defend the Faith.

First, there is an incredible growth and threat of non-Christian religious movements. A number of world religions are expanding within the U. S. The largest and most recent comprehensive study may be that done by the National Survey of Religious Identification (NSRI). This nationwide surveyed over 100,000 Americans in 1990 and conducted a similar survey in 2001. The results are quite revealing, the authors of the study conclude:

> The proportion of the population that can be classified as Christian has declined from eighty-six in 1990 to seventy-seven percent in 2001; . . . although the number of adults who classify themselves in non-Christian religious groups has increased from about 5.8 million to about 7.7 million, the proportion of non-Christians has increased only by a very small amount—from 3.3% to about 3.7 %; . . . the greatest increase in absolute as well as in percentage terms has been among those adults who do not

1. Barna Research Online, "Teenagers Embrace Religion but are not Excited about Christianity," [article on-line]; available from: http://www.barna.org/FlexPage.aspx?Page =BarnaUpdate&BarnaUpdateID=45; Internet; accessed 7 January 2005.

2. Barna Research Group, "Third Millennium Teens" (Venture: The Barna Research Group, 1999) as cited in Josh McDowell & Bob Hostetler, *Beyond Belief to Convictions* (Wheaton: Tyndale House, 2002).

> subscribe to any religious identification; . . . their number has more than doubled from 14.3 million in 1990 to 29.4 million in 2001; their proportion has grown from just eight percent of the total in 1990 to over fourteen percent in 2001. [3]

The significance of this observation is a clear decrease in the percentage of Christians as part of the total U. S. population and an increase among those that are non-Christian and those who do not classify themselves with any religion. Even if some of those not classified are Christians that do not want to reveal their religious affiliation (which is an interesting possibility in itself) there are some other concerns. Additional calculations done on these figures provided by Adherents.com reveals that the nonreligious or secular percentage of the U. S. population to be 13.2 percent. Islam and Buddhism were 0.5 percent and Hinduism was 0.4 percent. What is most reveling is the growth rate of these religions in the U. S. within a decade. Nonreligious growth is 110 percent, Islam is 109 percent, Buddhism is 170 percent, and Hinduism is 237 percent. In comparison Christianity, which includes all denominations, grew only 5 percent.[4]

3. Barry A. Kosmin, Egon Mayar and Ariela Keysar "American Religious Identification Survey 2001 The Graduate Center of the City University of New York," 2001, 10–11, http://www.gc.cuny.edu/faculty/research_briefs/aris.pdf [accessed May 17, 2007]

4. Adherents.com, "Largest Religious Groups in the United States of America" [data on-line]; available from: http://www.adherents.com/rel_USA.html; Internet; accessed 6 January 2005. This number may even be lower because the survey classified some cults (e.g., Mormons and Jehovah's Witnesses) as Christian denominations.

Religion	1990 Est. Adult Pop.	2001 Est. Adult Pop.	% of U. S. Pop., 2000	% Change 1990–2000
Christianity	151,225,000	159,030,000	76.5	+5%
Nonreligious/secular	13,116,000	27,539,000	13.2	+110
Judaism	3,137,000	2,831,000	1.3	-10
Islam	527,000	1,104,000	0.5	+109
Buddhism	401,000	1,082,000	0.5	+170
Agnostic	1,186,000	991,000	0.5	-16
Atheist	N/A	902,000	0.4	N/A
Hinduism	227,000	766,000	0.4	+237
Unitarian	502,000	629,000	0.3	+25
Wiccan/Pagan	N/A	307,000	0.1	N/A
Spiritualist	N/A	116,000		N/A
Native American	47,000	103,000		+119
Baha'i	28,000	84,000		+200
New Age	20,000	68,000		+240
Sikhism	13,000	57,000		+338
Scientology	45,000	55,000		+22
Humanist	29,000	49,000		+717

Table 3.1 Growth of Religions in the USA[5]

The NSRI survey that these numbers are taken from also reveals alarming growth pattern among other non-Christian religions. The New Age Movement includes a loosely connected web of groups unified by their acceptance of various Westernized Eastern religious thoughts. This grouping has grown 240 percent. The Humanists growth rate is the highest at over 700 percent. While the numbers of these groups compared to the total U. S. population are small, the growth rates are quite large.

5. Adapted from ibid. Used by Permission.

The number of cults[6] is estimated around 3000, which includes the involvement of millions of Americans.[7] Mormonism boasts the largest cult in the U. S. with over 2.6 million adherents. Jehovah's Witness follow with over 1.3 million.

A second threat includes critical attacks upon theistic truth. Attacks persist at both the scholarly and popular level. An example of the former is Michael Martin's *Atheism: A Philosophical Justification* and the latter is the so called "New Atheism" promoted by Richard Dawkins, Christopher Hitchens, Sam Harris, and Daniel Dennett.[8] While those considering themselves Atheist and Agnostic make up about 1 percent of the U. S. population, the Nonreligious/Secular is just above 13 percent of the U. S. population.[9] Atheism and skeptics provide some of the hardest objections to central questions of the Christian faith. Add to this the controversy between Evolution and Creation and the impact is evidenced by an ever increasing, yet subtle removal of God and religious freedoms in our society.[10]

---

6. The term "cult" is not intended to be pejorative. A cult can be defined sociologically and theologically. The latter identifies it as a group that claims to be Christian but denies one or more essential doctrines of the historic, orthodox Faith. The former indicates a religious or semi religious group whose members are controlled by a single individual or organization though authoritarian and manipulative means. See Norman L. Geisler & Ron Rhodes, When Cultists Ask (Grand Rapids: Baker, 1997), 9–18, and Ron Rhodes, *The Culting of America* (Eugene: Harvest, 1994).

7. For an index of these cults see Watchman Fellowship, Inc. "Watchman Fellowship's 2001 Index of Cults and Religions" [data on-line]; available from: http://www.watchman.org/cat95.htm. Internet; accessed 9 January 2005.

8. Michael Martin, *Atheism: A Philosophical Justification* (Philadelphia: Temple University Press, 1990. See also Martin's attempt to discredit Christian historical apologetics in Michael Martin, *The Case Against Christianity* (Philadelphia: Temple University Press, 1991). See Richard Dawkins, *The God Delusion* (New York: Houghton Mifflin, 2008); Sam Harris, *The End of Faith; Letter to a Christian Nation* (New York: W. W. Norton, 2004); Christopher Hitchens, *God Is Not Great: How Religion Poisons Everything* (New York: Hachette Book Group, 2007); and Daniel Dennett, *Breaking the Spell: Religion as a Natural Phenomenon* (New York: Penguin Group, 2006).

9. Unfortunately these categories were not carried in the NSRI 2001 survey and therefore growth or decline rates are not known.

10. A string of U. S. court decision indicates this starting in 1962 (Engle vs. Vitale) that banned class prayers from public schools; 1963 (Abington vs. Schempp) forbid class Bible reading; 1968 (Epperson vs. Arkansas) teaching against evolution was declared unconstitutional; 1980 (Stone vs. Graham) posting the Ten Commandments in classrooms was declared unconstitutional.

A third concern is the attacks on the historical truth of the Christian faith. In the 1990s it was the Jesus Seminar, a collection of liberal scholars who have met periodically over the last fifteen years and collectively produced two works that diminish the historical and theological value of the New Testament by claiming it is not historical regarding the words and works of the historical Jesus.[11] Individual members have authored several works expressing their individual views, some of which are even more radical than the group.[12] More recently a group of atheistic scholars lead by Robert Price has attacked the historicity of the resurrection.[13] Many of these scholars seem to make the headlines in numerous popular magazine and newspaper articles as well as television programs that often express their view as the consensuses of the "scholarly" community.

A fourth concern is more directly in the Church through false teaching. The Word-Faith movement promotes unbiblical practices and preaches a prosperity gospel. Words are considered a force that has creative abilities. If used correctly a faithful adherent is believed to be able to create their wealth and achieve godlike status.[14]

A fifth threat, religious pluralism, is the belief that all religions ultimately are on equal ground and worship the same God only in different ways, is quite popular. The Barna research group "Third Millennium Teens" reported that 63 percent of teens believe Muslims, Buddhists, Christians, and Jews pray to the same God. Forty-eight percent believe that it does not matter what religion you associate with because they all believe the same principles and truths. Fifty-eight percent believe all religious faiths teach equally valid truth. Fifty-six percent believe there is no way to tell which religion is true.[15] Most Americans reject the notion of absolute truth and believe that it does not matter to what God you pray because all religions are ultimately equal. In this view the choice of

11. See Robert W. Funk, Roy W. Hoover, et al. *The Five Gospels: What Did Jesus Really Say?* (New York: HarperCollins, 1993) and Robert W. Funk, et al. *The Acts of Jesus: What Did Jesus Really Do?* (New York: HarperCollins, 1998).

12. One example is John D. Crossan, *Who Killed Jesus?* (New York: Harper San Francisco, 1995).

13. Robert M. Price and Jeffery Jay Lowder, eds. *The Empty Tomb: Jesus Beyond the Grave* (New York: Prometheus Books, 2005).

14. For an evaluation of this movement see Hank Hanegraaff, *Christianity in Crisis* (Eugene: Harvest House, 1993).

15. Barna Research Group, "Third Millennium Teens" as cited in McDowell, *Beyond*, 9–10.

one religion over another is irrelevant because all faiths teach the same moral lessons about life.[16] Religious pluralism is quickly permeating even the Christian community.

Sixth, there is a disregard of both moral absolutes and truth in our society. Youth speaker Josh McDowell explains, "Our children are being raised in a society that has largely rejected the notions of truth and morality, a society that has somewhere lost the ability to decide what is true and what is right. Truth has become a matter of taste; morality has been replaced by individual preference."[17] Relativism is touted as the solution to how people with differing beliefs can "get along." The statistical study McDowell offers reinforces this observation. Seventy percent of churched and non-churched youth claim that absolute truth does not exist and that truth is relative.[18] Truth, morality, and religious preference are reduced to a personal choice or taste with no absolute implications for all people in the world. This mentality, that rejects any explanation of what constitutes absolute truth and reality, has come to be termed post-modernism.

Finally, a disregard for moral absolutes leads to a culture of moral relativity. Our society believes values are determined by our culture.[19] This is evidenced by the legalization of abortion which takes over a million innocent lives each year.[20] Likewise, there are ethical battles in society regarding euthanasia, homosexuality, and same-sex marriages. Our culture also continues a sometimes hidden emphasis on drugs, gambling, and sexual addiction. All of these are no doubt serious threats to the Christian educational process.

With such growing challenges to the Christian faith, it becomes more and more evident that simply teaching the content of the Bible

16. One popular presentation of this view can be found in John Hick, *A Christian Theology of Religions* (Louisville: Westminster John Knox Press, 1995).

17. Josh McDowell and Bob Hostetler, *Right From Wrong: What You Need to Know to Help Youth Make Right Choices* (Dallas: Word, 1994), 13.

18. Ibid., 14.

19. Although technically his view is a one-absolutist view Joseph Fletcher, *Situation Ethics: The New Morality* (Philadelphia: The Westminster Press, 1966) has been quite influential in American education by promoting this form of relativism.

20. From 1997–2001 the number of abortions was estimated at 1.3 million per year. Since 1973 it is estimated that there have been over 40 million abortions. National Right to Life, "Over 40 Million Abortions in U. S. since 1973" [data on-line]; available from: http://www.nrlc.org/abortion/aboramt.htm. Internet; accessed 20 January 2005.

in Christian secondary schools is not enough to preserve faith.[21] Given the current threats the future is likely to continue alone this same path wrapping the same old threats in new packages. The Scriptures acknowledge this point when they command believers to always "be ready" to defend the Faith (1 Pet 3:15; Jude 3).

EDUCATIONAL VALUE OF APOLOGETICS AT THE SECONDARY SCHOOL LEVEL

The vast majority, around 80 percent, of secondary Christian schools in the United States have discovered the need and value of including the study of Christian apologetics in their curriculum. There are several reasons to include apologetics at the secondary school level. First, apologetics provides the justification and clarification of the Christian world view. If one desires to prove to another that Christianity is true, there is no other subject than apologetics to turn. Hence, if Christian educators are concerned that their students are persuaded to accept the conclusion that Christianity is not true (or abandoning their faith), then only by giving instruction in the area of apologetics can this hope to be reversed. C. S. Lewis once commented,

> If all the world were Christian, it might not matter if all the world were uneducated. But, as it is, a cultural life will exist outside the Church whether it exists inside or not. To be ignorant and simple now—not to be able to meet the enemies on their own ground—would be to throw down our weapons, and to betray our uneducated brethren who have, under God, no defense but us against the intellectual attacks of the heathen. Good philosophy must exist, if for no other reason, because bad philosophy needs to be answered.[22]

Second, apologetics provides a foundation from which to build an understanding of our world and other subjects. As a student grows and develops, he or she is exposed to many seemingly new and challenging ideas in our world. Apologetics is a foundation and filter through which

21. This is not to suggest that the Bible should not play a foundational role in Christian education or that it is somehow insufficient to accomplish what it claims to be able to do (e.g., Heb 4:12). However, the challenges and questions faced by today's youth are not answered in the Bible alone, and therefore require as the Bible acknowledges (1 Pet 3:15; Jude 3), an apologetic for the faith.

22. C. S. Lewis, *The Weight of Glory* (New York: Collier Books, 1980), 28.

the student can pass new ideas to see if they are compatible with the Christian world view.

Third, apologetics provides the necessary answers to objections raised about the Christian faith. This may even hinder someone from becoming a Christian. One primary purpose that Scripture mentions for the use of apologetics is to "give an answer" (1 Pet 3:15). Studying apologetics can also serve a preparatory function by preparing the student to know what the questions are to which an answer must be given. Furthermore, it can help to resolve doubts the student may possess concerning the Faith.

Fourth, apologetics provides an understanding of the Christian faith by justifying and explaining its doctrinal beliefs. Not only can apologetics be used to know why we believe, but it can also demonstrate what is to be believed and why other beliefs should be rejected. In this way, apologetics can serve as a hedge against heretical and aberrant teaching that are constantly arising.[23] Giving reasons as to why Christian doctrine is true, enables a student to recognize false beliefs and know why they are false.

Fifth, apologetics is able to integrate other subjects of study. Because apologetics takes from such a broad range of subjects in order to justify Christian faith, it is possible to integrate the study of other subjects in apologetics. Hence, while apologetics may cover some difficult subjects, it is not so obscure of a subject that it cannot be connected with other subjects. This being the case it is possible to take what may be more familiar to the student and relate it to apologetics.

Finally, apologetics provides a foundation for the study of all other theological and biblical subjects. Seminaries have long recognized the need to do apologetics prior to doing theology or even studying the Bible. If there is no God, then there cannot be a word of God (Bible). If there is no absolute truth, then there cannot be an inerrant Bible. And if there is no meaning, then there cannot be communication from God or about God. Without meeting these kinds of preconditions, theological and biblical study cannot have a solid foundation of study. The sec-

---

23. This area in theology is known as polemics. The theological categories for what is incorrect are very precise and can include heretical, aberrant, suborthodox, unorthodox, and heterodox. For definitions and examples see Robert M. Bowman, Jr. *Orthodoxy and Heresy: A Biblical Guide to Doctrinal Discernment* (Grand Rapids: Baker, 1992).

ondary school would be wise to follow suit in providing the student an apologetic for other theological and biblical courses.[24]

APPROPRIATENESS OF APOLOGETICS IN THE SECONDARY SCHOOL

Apologetics at the secondary level seems to be the only place (or opportunity) to give every Christian student a systematic exposure to the subject. First Peter 3:15 reminds us that apologetics is for all Christians and Jude 3 informs us that our contention should be for "the faith" and not just a part of the Faith.

Some may suggest, however, that the church alone should be responsible for apologetic education. Certainly, the church should play a central role in apologetics and take seriously the biblical imperatives to train and prepare disciples to do apologetics.[25] Many Christian students do not attend Christian secondary schools and the church or home would be their only exposure to the subject. But with such staggering statistics, already discussed, regarding youth leaving the Faith over the past ten years, it is questionable as to whether the church or Christian home has lost its effectiveness in apologetics or is not teaching and reaching Christian students with apologetics. Peter Grant identifies one problem as "the minimal role of apologetics in most churches has led believers to feel that apologetics is an intrusion into the real ministry of the church. Whenever a pastor or church does something different from the average church . . . the innovation will be criticized."[26] Another consideration is that the nature of most church instruction does not require the measurement of educational objectives. Hence, there is really no way for the church to measure effectiveness, as most secondary schools are able to do. In short, the church may teach apologetics but it usually does not demonstrate effectiveness; while the Christian schools may demonstrate effectiveness but usually does not include apologetics as a systematic and distinct subject of study. Fifty-three percent of Christian schools teaching apologetics do not teach it as a distinct class. Instead, it is taught only as an integrated subject as a part of another class or subjects.[27]

---

24. In this way apologetics helps to serve as prolegomena to theology.

25. Ravi Zacharias and Norman Geisler, eds. *Is Your Church Ready? Motivating Leaders to Live an Apologetic Life* (Grand Rapids: Zondervan, 2003).

26. Peter J. Grant, "The Priority of Apologetics in the Church" in ibid., 55.

27. See Appendix A.

Another possibility includes Christian undergraduate programs. However, most undergraduate programs at Christian colleges, regardless of the major, do not require a course in apologetics to be taken. But even if they did, it would not capture the many Christian students who do not go on to college or attend vocational schools.

A further suggestion might be introducing the subject prior to the secondary level. However, this creates the problem of whether or not the student has mentally and physically matured enough to grasp the subject or benefit fully from its inclusion in the curriculum. There are two important areas of development needed to instruct secondary school children in a systematic course on apologetics. The first is reasoning ability and the second is moral development.

Reasoning Ability at the Secondary School Level

The subject of apologetics as a systematic subject of study requires the use of logic and abstract reasoning. This is not to suggest that there is no instruction to be given at the elementary level that could anticipate or help students with the subject or elements of apologetics.[28] But the nature of the subject matter covered in apologetics, suggests a fit with the intellectual and maturity level of the secondary school student.

Bärbel Inhelder and Jean Piaget were the first to do scientific research that would support this point. They concluded that "in the 7–11 year-old child, logic is applied only to concrete or manipulable objects. There is no operation available at this level which would make it possible for the child to elaborate an ideal which goes beyond the empirically given"[29] Yet,

28. One further concern about introducing apologetics, as a systematic subject of study, too early is the possibility of upsetting the faith a young child is able to express. At this level faith is usually one's acceptance of truth based on the authority of another (Parents, God, Bible, etc.). Trying to introduce logical arguments or constructs as proving something a child is unable to understand or comprehended may upset an important and biblical based structure of faith (Matt 18:3–6).

29. Bärbel Inhelder and Jean Piaget, *The Growth of Logical Thinking From Childhood to Adolescence: An Essay on the Construction of Formal Operational Structures*, trans. by Anne Parsons and Stanley Milgram (France: Basic Books, 1958), 348–49. Some Christian educators may object to the obvious humanistic world view of Piaget; however this point can stand independent of his world view because it is based on empirical observation and has been verified by other researchers. It does not require the Christian to accept his entire structure of moral and intellectual development which clearly does not include the concept or role of original sin. For a Christian assessment see Donald M. Joy, *Moral Development Foundations: Judeo-Christian Alternatives to Piaget/Kohlberg*

a wide range of experimental situations demonstrate that after a phase of development (11–12 to 13–14 years) the preadolescent comes to handle certain formal operations (implications, exclusion, etc.) successfully, but he is not able to set up an exhaustive method of proof. But the 14–15-year-old adolescent does succeed in setting up proofs . . . he systematically uses methods of control which require the combinatorial system . . . this structuring of the tools of experimental verification is a direct consequence of the development of formal thought and propositional logic.[30]

Hence, Inhelder and Piaget concluded that formal operational thought is attained about age fifteen. Others have followed and concluded similar results in logic and judgment.[31] Certainly the apologetics educator will see a range of intellectual ability at the secondary level and need to make adaptations in course material, content, and teaching methods.[32] But this evidence seems to suggest that the earliest and most appropriate time to introduce the student to apologetics, as a distinct and systematic subject of study, is in the secondary school around age fifteen.

Moral Development at the Secondary School Level

Another concern is the moral development of the child at this age. A course on apologetics will deal with and have to answer moral questions and dilemmas. Lawrence Kohlberg built a theory of moral development based on some of Piaget's theories and his own experimentation.[33] He identified three stages of development with sub stages that all people seem to progress through. Preconventional emphasizes the avoidance of punishments and getting rewards, conventional emphasizes the acceptance of social rules, and post conventional emphasizes moral principles. He based his theory on the experimental data that questioned children (ages 10, 13, and 16) concerning hypothetical stories that posed

---

(Nashville: Abingdon Press, 1983).

30. Inhelder, *Growth of Logical Thinking*, 347.

31. See the discussion by Kathleen S. Berger, *The Developing Person Through the Life Span*, 2d ed. (New York: Worth, 1988), 339–42.

32. This has been the experience of some who have attempted to teach apologetics at this age level. See Jeffrey L. Warren, "Training Youth Workers to Teach Youth Basic Christian Apologetics" (D.Min. project, Southwestern Baptist Theological Seminary, 1995), text-fiche.

33. Lawrence Kohlberg, *The Philosophy of Moral Development: Moral Stages and the Idea of Justice*, vol. 1 Essays on Moral Development (New York: Harper & Row, 1981).

ethical dilemmas. Subsequent research has sharply criticized his presuppositions, methodology, and results.[34] Additional research in the area
of moral development has concluded moral reasoning develops "in a
steady, gradual progression over the years."[35] Hence, the apologetics
educator will have to adapt to a possible wide range of moral reasoning ability and realize students at this level are in a process of developing these skills. It should also be viewed as an opportunity to influence
young minds with the Christian view of morality.[36] There should be no
objection to introducing moral issues and dilemmas as a part of a course
on apologetics. All adolescents go through moral development, the real
concern is who and what moral theory has influenced this development
the most. As indicated above, most youth, even Christian youth, are rejecting moral absolutes at alarming rates.[37]

Hence, with all the options exhausted, if apologetics is to be taught
to all Christian students, in a measurable and systematic manner, the
secondary Christian school is not only the best, but may be the only
option!

ANSWERING SOME OBJECTIONS

There are no doubt to be some objections raised that will be faced by
the apologetics educator concerning the implementation of a course in
Christian apologetics at the secondary school level. Over the years, I
have spoken with educators about apologetics and presented reasons for
a separate subject to be taught on apologetics. I have faced some of these
objections. Admittedly, they are not always expressed as "objections" as
many of them may just be concerns or even further questions. Hence,
the following might be asked when proposing such a course of study.

Apologetics is Not Taught in the Bible

Objection: Nowhere is the subject of apologetics formally taught in the
Bible as a subject? Furthermore, the Bible assumes the existence of God,
so why should we teach a subject that tries to prove God's existence?

---

34. See Berger, *Developing Person*, 347–50.

35. Ibid., 350.

36. See Norman L. Geisler, *Christian Ethics* (Grand Rapids, Baker, 1987).

37. McDowell, *Right From Wrong*, 260.

Answer: This question confuses the source of divine revelation with its defense. If we are to throw out apologetics because it is not formally taught in the Bible, then the same follows for almost any subject of Christian thought. There is no formal subject of theology, ethics, or counseling, etc. The fact is the Bible gives an imperative to do apologetics (Jude 3) and assumes that the subject of apologetics does exist since it affirms that we be ready or prepared to give an answer (1 Pet 3:15). Since there are many reasons for its contemporary need, as well as a biblical imperative, then Christian education should incorporate its study. While the Bible does not give us deductive arguments for God's existence, it does give reasons for believing in God (Rom. 1:18–20). These reasons rely on and respect the human ability to engage in rational thought. If human arguments do prove the existence of God, then we must incorporate them into our apologetics. Not to do so is to fail to allow humans to understand and use their God given rational ability. Not to teach these is to fail to educate the whole person.

Apologetics Does Not Work with Some People

Objection: Some people exposed to apologetics do not seem to be convinced. Even others, some who may be believers, also do not seem to be convinced nor have their doubts removed.

Answer: Even the Apostle Paul after using apologetics and preaching the gospel found, as recorded in Acts 17, faced three exhaustive options concerning a response "some began to sneer, but others said, 'We shall hear you again concerning this.' . . . But some men joined him and believed" (Acts 17:32–32). There is much more than rational thought involved in people who are making decisions regarding Christianity. Many have moral, family, or cultural issues involved in coming to understand truth. While we should not ignore these, neither should we use them as excuses to shy away from apologetics. To use the excuse of varied responses to our apologetic as a reason not to do apologetics is to ignore the biblical pattern. Furthermore, we cannot ignore that many believers and non-believers need rational answers, whether they realize it or not, to objections about Christianity. Since we are commanded in Scripture to be ready to give an answer, we should be obedient in our teaching apologetics and leave the results to God.

We Should Be Teaching Biblical World View, Not Apologetics

Objection: Students in Christian education need a biblical world view or more Bible and theology class than they need apologetics.

Answer: This question does make an important distinction between developing a biblical or Christian world view[38] and apologetics. Apologetics is the justification for the Christian world view. It is foundational to the development of a world view since it demonstrates the absolute truth of Christianity. World view education has become very important to a number of Christian educational programs. I am not opposed to this, but a world view does not justify itself, and to skip apologetics is to skip the justification of the Christian world view. The educator should not confuse or think that teaching the Christian world view is the same as teaching apologetics. Classes in Bible, theology, history, science, economics, etc. should all help a student develop an integrated Christian world view. But if apologetics is a distinct subject left out of the curriculum, then the Christian world view is left in mid air, with no foundation or justification. Hence, when students are having their world view challenged, undermined, or questioned, they will have learned no reasoned answer for why they believe.

No Room for Apologetics

Objection: Due to increased graduation requirements that are connected to college entrance requirements and/or state requirements, the curriculum for secondary schools is not flexible or is too crowded to offer a new course in apologetics.

Answer: Every Christian school and educator must seriously consider or weigh the options involved with implementing a new course of study. They must decide what they want to be the variable. If evidence exists that their students are abandoning the Faith or questioning its truthfulness, and the school decides not to change the curriculum to meet this problem, then the student has become the variable. The school must realize that if they are not willing to change in the area of curriculum to meet their student's needs, then their students will continue on the same path of rejection. If the times in which we live change and our

---

38. Some may make a distinction between the terms biblical and Christian world view. I prefer the latter due to its ability to include that God has revealed truth through general revelation or creation and special revelation or Scripture (Rom 1:19–20) which should be incorporated into one's world view (see Chapter 4).

curriculum does not change to meet the times, then our students will conform to the times in which we live. Furthermore, given the fact of a biblical imperative and strong societal indicator for the need to study apologetics, any decision to put state or college requirements ahead of the word of God is highly questionable.

The Church Alone Should Do Apologetics

Objection: The church, not the Christian secondary school, should be responsible for education in apologetics.

Answer: Actually, the imperative to do apologetics is not directed towards the church as an institution, but to the individual believer. Where apologetic training takes place is not mandated by Scripture, only that it takes place is implied in the mandate to give an answer (1 Pet 3:15). Hence, if an argument can be made that the secondary Christian school level is the best or most effective place in our culture to teach apologetics then that is where it should (not must) take place.

Apologetics Should Only Be Integrated

Objection: Apologetics should be integrated throughout the Bible program or secondary curriculum and therefore it is not necessary to devote a whole course of study to apologetics.

Answer: While it may be the case that most schools do integrate apologetics, it is questionable if any school can fulfill the biblical imperative of being systematic about providing an education to defend "the faith" (Jude 3) with this method. For example, it may be difficult to transfer any notion of a complete and systematic argument for the Christian faith with a fragmented exposure across other disciplines of study. The same is true for any course that just offers a question and answer approach to teaching apologetics. While this may be an acceptable approach for reinforcement of content or to show applications in other subjects, the overall effectiveness for achieving outcomes in apologetics is questionable. No other core subject in a Christian education program would expect to fulfill outcomes by this method. Having a separate course gives the subject much more legitimacy from the standpoint of all those involved. Discussing its history, vocabulary, ideas, controversies, testing, etc. over a sustained period with a starting and ending point gives the subject much more value, importance, and seriousness then integration alone. Furthermore, integration is usually left to teachers whose primary teaching expertise is in other subjects who may not have the necessary background, skills, and understanding of apologetics. Many who maybe asked to teach on the subject, including some Bible teachers, have never formally received instruction in the subject. Those who study the subject of apologetics on their own may miss a number of important aspects of the subject when it comes to its systematic expression and study.

Apologetics Is Too Difficult

Objection: Apologetics is too difficult of a subject to teach at the secondary level.

Answer: There are difficult areas in all subjects, and it is up to a competent teacher to deliver subject matter that is appropriate to the subject and level of students. Similar to most subjects there are degrees of difficulty in apologetics and most difficult areas can be broken done into simpler parts and explained.

No Qualified Teachers Exist

Objection: There are no qualified teachers either in apologetics or in education to teach the subject.

Answer: While this may have been the case in the past, and in some locations may still be the case, the career horizon for students with degrees or concentrations in apologetics is improving. Many educators teaching Bible courses at the secondary level are also able to get further training in apologetics even by staying in their current location and position through distant learning programs. Prior to the 1990s it was almost unheard of to find any evangelical Christian school in higher education offering a degree or concentration in apologetics.[39] Many colleges and even some seminaries did not even require a course in apologetics. In 1992, a Seminary started in Charlotte, North Carolina, that offered a 62 hour degree program that concentrated in apologetics. This Seminary, Southern Evangelical, first offered a Masters of Theological Study (M.Th.S.).[40] Later, the degree description changed to a Master of Arts in

39. Two exceptions to this are Simon Greenleaf School of Law 1980–1989 and Liberty University in the late 1980s, both offered a concentration in apologetics for their Master of Arts degrees.

40. *Southern Evangelical Seminary,* Catalog for 1992–93 School Year (Charlotte: Southern Evangelical Seminary, 1992), 14.

Apologetics (M.A.A.) and a divinity degree (M.Div. with Apologetics) was introduced.[41] In 1997 they added a master's degree, which is still available, through distance learning. Other schools have started degree programs offering a major or concentration in apologetics. Some accredited[42] schools include Biola University, Liberty University, Southeastern Baptist Theological Seminary, and Luther Rice Seminary. Southeastern and Southern Evangelical Bible College offer undergraduate degrees that emphasize or concentrate in apologetics.[43] Many other schools may offer degrees in philosophy, philosophy of religion, Christian thought or ideas, etc. that includes subjects directly or indirectly related to apologetics. Many of these schools depending upon their professors and theological persuasions may or may not embrace a classical approach to apologetics. Southern Evangelical is a Seminary and Bible College that can be described as maintaining a consistently classical approach to apologetics and an acceptance of moderate realism (i.e., Neo-Thomism) in its philosophy. This influence and emphasis is due to its co-founder Dr. Norman L. Geisler who has also served as Dean, President and professor of systematic theology and Christian apologetics. Dr. Geisler moved on in 2008 to co-found another school, Veritas Evangelical Seminary that maintains a similar emphasis in its degree programs.

No Teaching Materials Exist

Objection: There are few materials such as textbooks, curriculums, guides, and audio-video aids to accompany instruction.

Answer: This criticism is legitimate, especially as applied to apologetics in the secondary school. While apologetics is not a new subject, it is new to the secondary school level. There are some appropriate materials and many schools have successfully developed their own materials. When more schools begin to teach the subject, a market will emerge that

41. *Southern Evangelical Seminary*, Catalog 1996–98 (Charlotte: Southern Evangelical Seminary, 1996), 12. The M.Div. with Apologetics was actually introduced as an Addendum to the 1995–96 catalog.

42. Other non-accredited schools may offer similar degrees in name, but these schools listed offer accredited degrees. This means that the school is accredited by a regional, national, or professional accrediting agency recognized by the U. S. Department of Education and/or the Council for Higher Education Accreditation. See www.chea. org for a list of approved agencies and their schools.

43. This list is not intended to be a comprehensive list since many schools frequently add or drop degree programs and make other curriculum changes.

publishers will seek to fill a void with needed published materials to help teachers and students. The apologetics method and quality of material produced may vary greatly. But since there are a number of books and media materials on classical apologetics, this is not a valid excuse for avoiding a program in apologetics. Many teachers are able and gifted at adapting these materials for use at their teaching level. So while this criticism is legitimate, there are avenues around this, which should not prevent a CAE program from going forward. For a list of suggested materials, see Appendix B.

Apologetics Is Too Controversial

Objection: Apologetics is too controversial of a subject to introduce at the secondary school level. Not only will students disagree with the teacher, but also parents will not agree with what or how it is being taught.

Answer: Many things in the Christian community are controversial. It is impossible to avoid it. The fear of controversy should not be a reason against doing something the Bible commands. Most controversy that might develop will likely develop from misunderstandings. There are several things that a school system, teacher, and parents can do to clear the lines of communication and foster a clear presentation and need for apologetics to be taught in their school.

This justification is grounded in observations taken from our society that indicate the need for apologetics. Apologetics at the secondary school level provides not only the appropriate level for students but the only chance to impact every Christian with the benefits of teaching apologetics. It is worth emphasizing some negative factors that may develop or continue because of not implementing apologetics. First, a continued decline in the faith of youth and adults can be expected. While there may be other issues contributing to this alarming statistic, apologetics will not be given a chance to help reverse this. Second, current Christian youth will continue to experience decline in the ability to express a distinct intelligent Faith and answer to a growing anti-Christian culture. Hence, a failed biblical imperative exists or will exist in the Christian community.

QUESTIONS TO ANSWER

1. What are some struggles you believe a teacher might face trying to teach classical apologetics to young students for the first time?

2. What needs exist among your students that could be met by teaching apologetics?

3. Create a list of objections to teaching apologetics and write out your responses to them?

SELECT READINGS

Norman L. Geisler, "The Need for Defending the Faith."

Josh McDowell, *Beyond Belief to Convictions*, chapter 1.

4

World Views and Christian Education

OBJECTIVES

Recognize the Christian world view as it applies to Christian education.

Distinguish between world view education and Christian apologetics education.

THE PRECEDING CHAPTERS ESTABLISHED that apologetics has an important and distinct history as a Christian discipline of study (Chapter 1) and should be approached, especially for educational purposes, according to the classical method (Chapter 2). It also has justification to be taught at the secondary school level (Chapter 3). The purpose of this chapter is to cover elements needed in a philosophy of Christian education that are important to understanding the role of apologetics and its incorporation as a distinct subject of study.

To accomplish this we first show the means by which the Christian world view is rationally justified and further developed an understanding of God's revelation. Then we explore the Christian educational view by contrasting it with two opposing world views. Finally, in this chapter, we distinguish apologetics from a worldview education. In the next two chapter, we consider important subjects of study that support and relate to the teaching of apologetics, which are needed to properly move toward a Christian philosophy of education for teaching apologetics.

There is usually a sequence to the development of curriculum. An educational philosophy develops out of one's world view. The curriculum develops and follows out of one's educational philosophy (Figure 4.1). Hence, we will first consider the justification of the Christian world view.

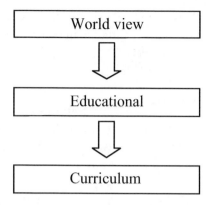

Figure 4.1 Development of Educational Philosophy

GOD'S REVELATION

A Christian world view that is to be educationally sound must reject any opposing world view. Apologetics gives the Christian educator the foundation, justification, and clarification for this assertion. There are several excellent texts on apologetics from the classical position. These clearly defend the Christian world view against all opposing world views.[1] To establish the Christian world view one must validly argue for its truth on universally accepted grounds. This argument must be comprehensive and systematic (see Appendix C). It must culminate in a demonstration that the Bible, alone, is the inspired and written word of God. Only then can the Christian thinker have an unshakable foundation to develop and express a truly Christian world view.

From the Bible we discover that God has revealed true knowledge in two spheres or realms of inquiry: General and special revelation. General revelation refers to God's creation including the universe, nature, and human nature and activities (Ps 19:1–6; Rom 1:19–20). General revelation is broader than special revelation in that it covers truth in all human subjects of inquiry and practice, such as science, history, math, human government and the arts. It even serves as the basis for the subject of apologetics itself. Norman Geisler states in his *Systematic Theology*, "General revelation is integral to Christian apologetics, since it is the data with which theists construct arguments for the existence of

---

1. See the popular book Norman Geisler and Frank Turek, *I Don't Have Enough Faith to Be an Atheist* (Wheaton: Crossway Books, 2004). For a more advanced approach, see Norman L. Geisler, *Christian Apologetics* (Grand Rapids: Baker, 1976).

God. . . . Without it there would be no basis for apologetics."[2] If God had not revealed himself in creation and human nature, then the traditional cosmological, design and moral arguments would not be possible.

Special revelation refers to the sixty-six canonical books of the Bible (2 Tim 3:16–17; John 10:35).[3] Humans can legitimately pursue inquiry of both realms of revelation expecting to discover truth about God and the created world. Both revelations are from God. Hence, there is complete agreement or harmony between Scripture and the created world, since both have the same infallible source: God. However, humans are limited and fallible, their inquiries and interpretations of the two revelations can be in disagreement and error (see Figure 4.2). Broadly speaking, the two descriptions given to the subjects of human inquiry are Science and Theology. The subjects for educational purposes, however, are often integrated and subdivided. The scientific study may include the hard sciences (physics, chemistry, and biology), humanities, and technologies. Theology may be systematic, historical, biblical, etc.

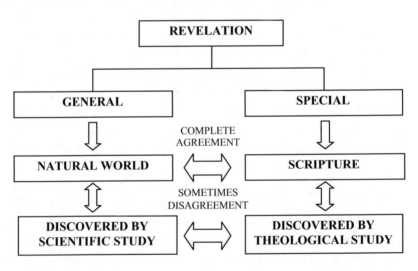

Figure 4.2 Relationship between General and Special Revelation

2. Norman L. Geisler, *Introduction Bible*, Vol. 1 of *Systematic Theology* (Minneapolis: Bethany House, 2002), 65.

3. While it is debated in Christendom (especially with Roman Catholics) whether revelation should be limited to these books alone, all Christian's agree that it should at least include them. For a Protestant defense see Norman L. Geisler and Ralph E. MacKenzie, *Roman Catholicism: Agreements and Differences* (Grand Rapids: Baker, 1995), 157–75.

Educators should be aware of investigations and discoveries of both realms. While the world view of the human inquirer is important, it may be the case, as Louis LaBar recognized in 1958, that "throughout history unbelievers have continually found intriguing new insights into man's behavior because they have taken pains to study God's creature."[4] Hence, we are on good grounds to ask and answer the question: What can be found in general and special revelation that should be a part of an educational philosophy that supports the inclusion of apologetics as a distinct subject of study?

EDUCATIONAL WORLD VIEWS

A world view "is a conceptual framework or 'system' of thought through which everything is given meaning and context."[5] Foundational to this system of thought is one's view of God. Philosophically there are several world views to consider.[6] However, there are only three major world views trying to make a distinct influence on a philosophy of education in our society: Theism, Atheism, and Pantheism. The Christian world view is Theism.[7] This is the belief that there is a transcendent God who created the world and acts or intervenes in the world. Atheism is the belief that there is no God or gods. The religion of Atheism is humanis-

4. Louis E. LaBar, *Education That is Christian* (Old Tappan: Fleming H. Revell, 1958), 50.

5. Norman L. Geisler, "Some Philosophical Perspectives on Missionary Dialogue," in *Theology and Mission*, ed. David J. Hesselgrave (Grand Rapids: Baker, 1978), 242.

6. Other world views include Deism, the belief that there is a transcendent God that chooses not to intervene (through miracles) in the world. Panentheism is the belief that God has two poles (bi-polar) in that he is the world (finite) and has an immaterial part that is beyond the world (infinite). Another way to think of this view is that God has a body (world) and a soul (immaterial spirit). Finite Godism is the belief that God is limited; hence he is not infinite or omnipotent. Polytheism is a sub category of Finite Godism which holds that there are many gods. In addition to these world views there are some methodologies (e.g., agnosticism, skepticism) that may present themselves as if they are a way of life or kind of world view. For an apologetic towards these world views see Norman L. Geisler, *Christian Apologetics* (Grand Rapids: Baker, 1976).

7. It should be acknowledged that two other major religions are theistic (i.e., Judaism, Islam). However, Christianity argues for a superior source of revelation (the New Testament) that contradicts one (Islam-Qur'an) and fulfills the other (Judaism-Hebrew Bible). For an apologetic towards these religions see Norman L. Geisler and Abdul Saleeb, *Answering Islam: The Crescent in Light of the Cross*, 2d ed. (Grand Rapids: Baker, 2002) and Michael L. Brown, *Answering Jewish Objections to Jesus* (Grand Rapids: Baker, 2000–2003).

tic. Pantheism is the belief that God is the world (or the world is God). Eastern religions and the popular New Age movement in the West are Pantheistic. Obviously, with such differing views of God, each world view will express a different approach and understanding of education. It will be valuable to look at some major areas of education and how each world view presents a different view. Each view as we present it should be understood as the logical outworking of the world view and not necessarily representative of every educator that may hold the world view.

Theism-Christian

Christians believe that *human* beings are a soul-body unity that is conceived in a sin nature that is passed down from an original fallen state. Hence, as *students* grow and develop they have a bent towards evil and selfishness. *Discipline* should be structured to acknowledge, control, and correct this nature through appropriate means. However, the only ultimate solution to the problem is salvation through Jesus Christ, which results in a new capacity to do good that is glorifying to God. The *teacher* is an authority[8] figure for the student and both must make their *objective* a Christ-centered relationship (i.e., a proper relationship with Jesus Christ) for true education to take place. The *teaching process* involves not only the teacher and student but also acknowledges and involves the Holy Spirit. The *focus of education* and learning takes place in four areas: cognitively (mind), affectively (emotions), spiritually (soul), and psychomotor (skills). Education is a change or growth in all these areas. The *source of truth* for a Christian is God who has revealed himself in the two realms of general and special revelation. *Truth and morals* (values) are absolute and their source is God who has revealed them as part of natural law and Scripture. The *ultimate goal* of the student and education is to glorify God.

Atheism-Humanism

Humanists are materialists that do not acknowledge a soul (or immaterial aspect of humanity). They believe students are intrinsically good in nature and the problem to overcome is ignorance. Discipline may be

---

8. There is an important distinction to make between authoritarian and an authoritative teacher. The latter is Christian in the sense that the teacher is prepared to teach knowledge and truth. The former is not Christian since it ignores the needs and free will of the student which can stifle learning.

more permissive because it does not acknowledge any intrinsic evil in the student. The teacher is understood more as a facilitator or guide than as a source of authority to the student. The overall objective is centered on world or societal improvement. The teaching process only acknowledges a relationship between the student and teacher. The focus of education only concerns cognitive, affective, and psychomotor aspects. The source of truth is relative to the culture. Morals or values are invented by society. The ultimate goal of education is to improve society.

Pantheism-New Age

New Age advocates emphasize the spirit or soul over the body and believe that humans are divine or (God). The problem for the student is to overcome unenlightenment. Hence, discipline must be self-imposed or come from within the student to be successful. The teacher is a spiritual guide (or Guru) that helps the student reach their potential for divinity. The educational objective is centered on human self-improvement. The teaching process is self-enlightenment. The focus of education is on the spiritual to the extreme of denying the cognitive, affective, and psychomotor aspects. The source of truth is within the student's own divinity which needs to be realized. Truth is therefore relative to the individual and values are created by the individual. The ultimate goal of education is the realization of individual divinity or a global new world order.

	THEISM	ATHEISM	PANTHEISM
GOD	One Transcendent God	No God	All is God
RELIGION	Christianity	Humanism	New Age
HUMANS	Bent Towards Evil	Good	God
STUDENT'S CONDITION	Fallen	Ignorant	Unenlightened
DISCIPLINE	Structured	Permissive	Self-Imposed
TEACHER	Authority	Facilitator	Guide
OBJECTIVE	God-Centered	World-Centered	Human-Centered
TEACHING PROCESS	Involves Teacher-Student-God	Involves Teacher-Student	Involves Student-Teacher

	THEISM	ATHEISM	PANTHEISM
FOCUS OF EDUCATION	Cognitive, Affective, Spiritual, Physical	Cognitive, Affective, Physical	Spiritual
SOURCE OF TRUTH	From God	From World	From Within
TRUTH	Absolute	Relative (To Culture)	Relative (To Individual)
VALUES	Revealed	Invented (By Society)	Created (By Self)
ULTIMATE GOAL	Glorify God	Improve Society	Self Divinity/ New World Order

Table 4.1 Educational World Views Compared[9]

APOLOGETICS AND CHRISTIAN WORLD VIEW EDUCATION

Earlier (chapter 3) we briefly answered an objection that suggested we should teach a biblical or Christian world view course instead of apologetics. As if somehow a Christian world view incorporates, all that apologetics has to offer us. As I stated before, there is nothing wrong with teaching a Christian world view. However, the two are distinct subjects because apologetics justifies the Christian world view. While one may incorporate aspects of apologetics into the teaching of the Christian world view and vise versa, they are not the same. In fact, some have even criticized world view education for doing nothing but apologetics. Professor David Scott recently commented, "Pick up any book on worldview and thumb through its contents. Read any worldview conference schedule . . . Here is what you find: ninety percent of the content of what we call Christian worldview is actually apologetics. That means that almost all of our focus and energy in worldview is targeted exclusively at refuting other people's worldviews."[10]

---

9. Norman L. Geisler *Apologetics in Christian Educational Ministry* (class notes, Charlotte, NC: Southern Evangelical Seminary, 2002). Copyright © Norman L. Geisler, used by permission.

10. David Scott, "A Church without a View: Jonathan Edwards and Our Current Lifeview Discipleship Crisis." *Christian Apologetics Journal* 7, no. 2 (2008): 29.

When one examines what is offered as apologetics under the name "world view," the situation is actually worse for the educational apologist. For example, some texts on a Christian world view only refer to arguments for God's existence. David Noebel's popular secondary text on world views, which is probably most often used for apologetic courses (see Appendix A), gives only brief attention to the moral and design arguments. The other arguments do not fair any better with only a brief definition.[11] But this hardly gives their full expression or implication and usually never connects the demonstrating of God's existence and nature with the same God described in Scripture. Furthermore, there is little room given to God's general revelation. Noebel believes: "General revelation has been viewed consistently . . . by a variety of Christian theists as a necessary but insufficient means for providing knowledge about the Creator and His Character." This causes him to conclude, "It is better theology and philosophy to begin with the God of the Bible to explain the universe than to begin with the universe to explain God."[12] This may or may not work well for an approach to comparing world views, but it will not do for teaching classical apologetics. It certainly was not the apostle Paul's method, who clearly started with nature when he said, "For since the creation of the world His invisible attributes, His eternal power and divine nature, have been clearly seen, being understood through what has been made, so that they are without excuse (Rom 1:20).

Such an approach to world views usually, at best, compares and contrasts other views with the Christian view. In doing so they create a presuppositonal picture that can only compare the true view with false views in certain areas. It is still left to educational apologist to present a systematic argument that one view is true (i.e., the Christian view) and the other views are false, thus adjudicating between the views.

What a world view education course should do, which is different than apologetics, is teach the process and result of how to integrate

11. David A. Noebel, *Understanding the Times*, 2nd ed. (Manitou Springs CO: Summit Press, 2006), 45, 498. The first edition did give fuller expression to the cosmological argument see David A. Noebel, *Understanding the Times* (Manitou Springs CO: Summit Press, 1991), 181. But even here, there is no direct connection made with the argument and the God of Scripture.

12. Noebel, *Understanding*, 2nd ed., 44. Again, the first edition added a footnote saying, "This does not mean . . . that one cannot point to general revelation as good evidence for the existence of God." Noebel, *Understanding*, 107. But even this admission only comes close to the role such argument should have in classical apologetics.

God's general and special revelation to develop distinctively Christian views on various subjects and topics. It should also show the life implications and application of doing this. A world view teacher may have to narrow the selection of topics and decide what is the most important or central to a distinct Christian view to learn about. Many areas and views will likely overlap other subjects taught in the school curriculum. Noebel's text includes theology, philosophy, ethics, biology, psychology, sociology, law, politics, economics, and history.[13] There are, no doubt, areas a Christian needs to express a distinct view on such as technology, medicine, or education.[14] These may be considered less important, but the point is that none of this is rightly to be called apologetics or considered the same as teaching Christian apologetics.

There are important subjects the educator must gain a proper understanding of to support a classical approach to apologetics. Each of these subjects requires an insight to their nature and appropriate methodology needed for investigating their subject of study. Apologetics, as subject of study, will delve into and cross several subjects to build a case for Christianity. Some of these briefly include philosophy, mathematics, literature, biblical studies, etc. (see page 146 Table 8.2). A proper investigation into various subjects demands that the appropriate methods be used to explore a subject of study in order to discover truth. Aristotle seems to be the first to identify this necessity: "It is a mark of an educated man to look for precision in each class of things just so far as the nature of the subject admits: it is evidently equally foolish to accept probable reasoning from a mathematician and to demand from a rhetorician demonstrative proofs."[15] One should not expect the certainty found in mathematical conclusion to be the same as that found in historical conclusions. The differing nature of these subjects will yield differing levels of certitude. Hence, the principle of having a method appropriate to the nature of the subjects, although quite simple, is very important.

God has revealed himself through general (i.e., creation) and special (i.e., Scripture) revelation. Both are legitimate human venues

---

13. Noebel, *Understanding*, 2nd ed., 44.

14. Due to the technological advancements in various fields, there are actually many issues that have not clearly been thought through or expressed from the standpoint of a Christian world view.

15. Aristotle, *Nicomachean Ethics*, in vol. 2 Jonathan Barnes, ed., *The Complete Works of Aristotle* (Princeton: Princeton University Press, 1984), 1094b24.

of investigation and discovery. As a result, a Christian educator is on good ground to integrate truth found in both areas into a philosophy of education, which can properly be called Christian. This Christian view is justified by the very subject of apologetics, which should not be confused in the educational curriculum with other subjects such as a course on world views.

QUESTIONS TO ANSWER

1. Distinguish between general and special revelation.

2. Distinguish the understanding that education has in the Christian world view from other world views.

3. How is teaching Christian apologetics different from teaching a Christian world view.

SELECT READINGS

David A. Noebel, *Understanding the Times.*

Norman L. Geisler, *Christian Apologetics*, part 2.

5

Toward a Philosophy of Christian Education for Apologetics: General Revelation

OBJECTIVES

Define the role arguments for God's existence should play in teaching apologetics.

Differentiate between the nature of philosophical subjects and historical subjects as they relate to teaching apologetics.

T HIS CHAPTER ADMITTEDLY COVERS some topics of a more philosophical nature that some may find difficult. These, however, are important, as we will see, to the teaching of apologetics. To move towards a proper philosophy of education for a classical apologetic, we will lay the foundation and proper methodology for some of the most fundamental subjects needed for teaching apologetics. These include truth, metaphysics, epistemology, natural theology, science, history, and education.

TRUTH

We will begin with the foundational subject of truth. Frank Gaebelein, a well known Christian educator influentially asserted: "A Christian education has a holy obligation to stand for and honor the truth wherever it is found."[1] Hence, the assertion that "all truth is God's truth"[2] would seem to satisfy a discussion on truth related to general revelation. Even

1. Gaebelein, *The Pattern of God's Truth*, 23.
2. Ibid., 20.

this acknowledgement is found in special revelation in the words of the Apostle Paul, "whatever is true . . . let your mind dwell on these things." (Phil 4:8). However, a post-modern notion of relativistic truth is quite common, even among Christians. Is truth absolute or relative? This question is very important to the subject of apologetics. After all, if truth is relative then choosing one world view or religion over another is no more significant then choosing one ice cream flavor over another. The whole enterprise of teaching or doing apologetics rests on the notion that some things are true and other things are false, and this must be absolutely true for everyone everywhere. Hence, it is necessary to defend first the absolutistic nature of truth against relativism. The notion of a relative truth is quite popular and can be understood in two ways.[3] It can be relative to time and place or relative to persons. Absolute truth is understood as a claim that if true for one person it is true for everyone regardless of time and place. If it is true at one time and in one place, it is true for all times and all places. A relativist, for example, would claim that the statement "Ronald Regan is president" is only true for a certain time (1980–1989) and place (USA) and is not now true. Hence, such truth is relative to time, place, and persons. However, the relativists does not realize that what is true at one time, one place, and for only some persons is really always true and true for all. That "Ronald Regan is president," said in the 1980s, is true for everyone and every place and it will never not be true. It is true today that Regan was president in the 1980s and that will never not be true.

The same analysis follows for personal statements such as "I feel cold" (said on a certain date) is true for everyone and everywhere that "I feel cold" (on a certain date). It is important to recognize what is being claimed to be true. It is not being claimed that everyone feels cold. Likewise, some ancient human may have said, "I believe the earth is flat." If so, it will always be true for all people that some ancient human believed in a flat earth. It does not mean it was true in ancient times that the earth is flat and it is false now (because we know the earth is round). False beliefs, even though they are false, may be believed nonetheless. What is true is that they are believed, and this must be absolute.

My professor once challenged the class by saying he would give ten dollars to anyone that could come up with a relative truth. After a few feeble attempts by students, it was clear that he would keep his money.

3. Geisler, *Introduction Bible*, 119–20.

Truth claims by definition must be absolute. It might come as a surprise, even to some Christians, that there is no such thing as a relative truth. The vary nature of truth demands that it be absolute. If it is true at all, it is true everywhere, all the time, and for everyone, even through its application or claim may be limited. Furthermore, relativism is prone to self-defeating claims. The claim that "all truth is relative" relies on the notion of absolute truth to support itself. In other words, it cannot be a relative truth that all truth is relative. For the claim to be true there must be absolute truth, which of course would make the claim false. This self defeating nature of a relative truth especially when applied to education results in the absurd. If truth is relative, one could never know that they learned anything that is true for everyone. It could only be said that it is true to the person and place. No one could truly know if they rightly or wrongly answer a question on a test. Learning itself becomes immeasurable in any absolute sense and knowing anything for sure becomes impossible if truth is relative. Hence, relative truth leads to a self-defeating system and educational skepticism.

There are several theories of truth. However, they can easily be divided into correspondent theories and non-correspondent theories. Truth can be found only in a correspondence view. That is, as observed by Norman Geisler, "Truth is what corresponds to its object (referent), whether this object is abstract or concrete. As applied to the world, truth is the way things really are."[4] Additionally, Mortimer Adler (1902–2001) reminds us that,

> The correspondence theory asserts (1) that there is a reality independent of the mind, and (2) that truth (or, what is the same thing, knowledge) exists in the mind when the mind agrees with, conforms or corresponds to, that independent reality. When what I assert agrees with the way things really are, my assertions are true; otherwise they are false. . . . The principle of noncontradiction is both an ontological principle (the principle that contradictories cannot coexist in reality) as well as a logical rule (the rule that thinking cannot be correct if it is self-contradictory).[5]

All other views of truth are non-correspondence and are ultimately self-defeating because they must rely on the correspondence view to assert that a different view of truth should be accepted. For example if

4. Ibid., 114.
5. Adler, *Intellect*, 98–99.

I have a different theory of truth (which denies correspondence) and I want to assert this theory of truth is true, then I am relying on the correspondence view of truth to say: Namely that my different theory corresponds to the way things are; even though my different theory denies correspondence. This is not to say that other theories do not posses some value or insight into the nature of truth. But ultimately, the correspondence theory prevails because it alone is not self-defeating.

Finally, the nature of truth is the same for all disciples or subjects. Many may affirm correspondence when disputing a financial transaction, but then want truth to be subjective when choosing a religion that is "true" for them. However, the nature of truth does not allow this, and if Christianity is true, then all non-Christianity is false.

METAPHYSICS

A philosophy of education should begin by deciding the most basic question of existence and reality. This is properly identified as the subject of metaphysics, which is the study of being or reality itself: every other subject studies being as some *thing*, but metaphysics studies being as being. A wrong answer at this level of inquiry can drastically affect the understanding and role of apologetics. If things in reality are unknowable what is the use in teaching argumentation and providing evidence that supposedly proves Christianity? Hence, a Christian philosophy of education should avoid the philosophical extremes of Idealism, such as that espoused by Immanuel Kant and Naturalism represented in David Hume. Idealism stresses minds and ideas as the essence of humanity to the exclusion of an external knowable physical world. Naturalism stresses the natural or material to the exclusion of spiritual or non-material things. However, we will present a middle ground that preserves a knowable material and immaterial (i.e., spiritual) reality in agreement with the Christian world view.

So, what does it mean to be real? Notice that this question is not asking if there is reality or if we know reality? The student in an apologetics class already knows reality. They first discovered this when they were infants. However, the method that one uses to answer this question is important. For example, the modern Cartesian understanding, which is based in the philosophy of René Descartes, attempts to prove the existence of an external world by starting with thought: "I think, therefore

I am." However, as philosopher Ralph McInerny demonstrates, this is clearly a mistaken approach,

> The Cartesian method arrives at the claim that the self is prior to the world, that our certainty of our own existence is greater than our certainty that the world exists. Indeed, we arrive at certainty of the existence of God *and then* derive from features of God the reliability of knowledge for the world. . . . [In contrast the moderate realism understands that] Everyone knows for sure things about the world; things whose existence cannot be coherently doubted. The things of the world are what we first know, and we become aware of ourselves insofar as we know the world. . . . Philosophy is not the study in which we for the first time come to know things for sure. Philosophy presupposes that we are already in possession of truth about the world and ourselves.[6]

As one of my professors, Dr. Richard Howe, once said in class, "If the brick wall does not convince you that it is real, what makes you think a philosophical argument will convince you it is real?" Professor Howe is not saying there is no philosophical description that can made that accurately reflects on how we know being. But that philosophy itself must begin with being and not anywhere else. This is because being or the existence of reality is undeniable. If one asserts that, "There is no such thing as reality," one assumes the real existence of that statement about reality in order to make the assertion. Hence, our original question is more important and appropriate: What does it mean to be real?

Thomas Aquinas helps us answer this question by understanding being or what it means to exist. Take a walk to your nearest forest and stop to observe the first tree you see. If you observe the tree long enough, you will notice some things about the tree. First, that it exists! This may be obvious but it is quite profound since there is nothing immediately evident that makes the tree exist verses not existing. Second, over time you will notice that the tree changes. It grows taller and changes color throughout the year. Third, you will also notice that the tree you are observing is not the same as other things. It is not the same as the large rock, the grass, or the water near by. If you even observe it closely enough, you will notice that it is even different from all the other trees. Aquinas insists that these observations reveal principles about being. He says

---

6. McInerny *A First Glance at St. Thomas Aquinas*, 32, 34. This is the core distinction between Cartesian and Moderate Realist method.

being is composed of existence (that it is existing) and essence (what it is e.g., a tree). His term for something that exists is act or actuality (existence) and his term for the fact that it changes is potency (capacity to change). Thus, it is possible to have different kinds of being in terms of their act and potency. Aquinas goes on to observe that nothing that is composed of act and potency can account for its own existence or capacity to change. Why?

For something to exist it must be either 1) caused by itself, 2) uncaused or 3) caused by another. There are no other options. We can cross off the first one caused by itself. Self causation is impossible. It would have to exist prior to itself to cause its own existence. Uncaused also must be crossed off our list. After all, we have already seen that it exists. So therefore, it must be caused by something else. But what about that something else; must it also be composed of act and potency. Maybe, but Aquinas would tell us that there must be something that exists that has no potency in order to account for a world filled with existing things that have act and potency. There must be something that is pure act, without any potency or capacity for change. Something that is uncaused, but able to account for all the things needing a cause.

Hence, there must be something that is pure actuality with no potentiality. There can only be one Being that is pure Act. That is, one Being where what it is (essence) and that it is (existence) are identical. Every other being *has* being and is composed of act and potency. Since there can be different kinds of beings (those composed of act/potency) there must also be one Being that *is* Being or pure Actuality.

EPISTEMOLOGY

So, how do we know? Notice, we are not asking the question, Do we know or can we know? It seems quite clear that we know, for to deny this affirms the self-defeating nature of skepticism. In answering this, we must avoid the problems evident in critical realism and idealism. Both views always begin with thought, and try to argue to the existence of an external world. If thought unsuccessful the result is idealism, if thought successful then realism. But the existence of a real world is already evident to us and therefore does not need to be proved. As Frederick Wilhelmsen shows us: "*Man knows there are things because he senses them.*"[7] From the time

---

7. Wilhelmsen, *Man's Knowledge of Reality*, 31, emphasis his.

we are infants we know all kinds of things even without much thought involved. But to answer the question how do we come to know will take some thought. As we will see, our answer to the question will also give us a glimpse into the very nature of reality and humanity.

It will help to observe reality again and consider a well known problem in philosophy: Universals. These are categories or concepts that contain every item of a class (sometimes called genes or species). For example, consider our example of a real tree. What makes us classify it as a tree? Any one quality of a tree considered in isolation such as its colors (brown and green), its height (twenty feet), its trunk, branches, and leaves does not constitute the classification of a tree, but put them together and that is what it is. This is because all the objects that meet the qualities of a tree are universally recognized as this particular concept or category which also excludes all other classes. However, we experience only particular instances of *this* tree or *that* tree. We never find *the* "ideal" or universal class of a tree in reality apart from its expression in a particular tree. Yet, at the same time, we create from the particular its universal class and call it what it is. The perennial problem of universals is: Are these universals real? How we answer this question will directly affect our answer to the question of how we know reality.

Four answers have been given to the question of universals: 1) Absolute Realism says universals exist in themselves (Plato); 2) Conceptualism says universal exist as categories in the mind with no relation to things outside the mind (Kant); and 3) Nominalism denies any universals outside or inside the mind.[8] However, only 4) Moderate Realism[9] reveals a path to how we know by explaining that universals are grounded in reality by virtue of the forms or essense of things and can come really to exist in the intellect. Physical objects exist independently and they do not depend on our mental processes to exist. In other words, there is a real external world that can be known. We must recognize that the problem is more than a logical one. It is primarily metaphysical. Universals must apply to every particular or it is not a universal and they (universals) can have a form of existence in the mind of a knower.

---

8. For a nominalist words become empty abstractions because there is no reality to the thing only a name. Universal ideas are not ontologically real.

9. "Moderate" in realism is to designation the position that holds universals really do come to exist in the intellect, but their existence stops there (moderate).

Because of the problem of universals, only Moderate Realism is able to account for how we can really know reality.

As we have said, all finite beings are composites of actuality (existence) and potentiality (to change). Existence or *esse* is the act by which an essence (what something is) has being. Again, these are principles in a being and not things in themselves. An essence is further composed of substance and accidents. For example, a human being is a substance.[10] But the fact that he or she is a certain color, height, weight, etc. is accidental to the substance. Accidents do not exist apart from substances. You cannot, for example, find the color white apart from a substance. Accidents can change; such as a human who tans in the sun undergoes a color change. Substances cannot undergo this kind of change. A human essence cannot become a cat essence or vise versa. The substance is that which remains the same even though accidental qualities may change through time. We know substances through our five senses of seeing, smelling, hearing, tasting, and touching.

A substance can be further, explained, by the relationship of form and matter. This is how we come to know substances in reality.[11] The form of something is related to its actuality; form is what something is (i.e., an essence). For example, a cat has the form of catness, and a dog has the form of dogness. Matter is related to the individual potentiality (to change). It is that which individuates an essence to be this cat (or that cat). Matter, as used here, should not be equated with physical matter, and form should not be equated with the shape of something. Instead, these are principles of finite substances in reality. The form of a substance is immaterial. The matter of a substance is what individuates the essence to be a particular thing (that gives it extension in space) which is limited to its individualized form. We can say a dog is not a cat because of their different form or essence. We can say this cat is not that cat because

10. Substance should not be confused with subsistence. Something can have subsistence with no subject. The classification of genes and species for example has subsistence and does not require a subject in which to exist. Likewise, "humanity" is a subsistent reality but it does not have to have a substance.

11. In Aquinas' own words: "Now in a material thing there is a twofold composition. First there is the composition of form with matter; and to this corresponds that composition of the intellect whereby the universal whole is predicated of its part: for the genus is derived from common matter, while the difference that completes the species is derived from the form and the particular from individual matter" (Aquinas, *Summa Theologica*, 1a 85, a 5).

of their different matter. The way in which we know something is by its form, which is united to matter. We know a substance (individual form/matter) via our five senses which data is put together and processed by our internal senses. Since the form of a substance is immaterial, it is able to enter our mind and we are able to know the substance as it is in itself. Our intellect is able to abstract the universal from the individualized form.

It is very important to understand that the form, which enters the mind, is not a different substance or copy of the substance that is outside the mind. The same form that is united with matter outside the mind unites with the mind of the knower. In a sense the knower and the thing known become one and is therefore not something subject to physical or scientific examination. This view avoids Cartesian/Kantian representationalism and idealist epistemology that shifts the knowing of things to the consciousness of the mind rather than the thing in itself and a purely naturalistic view that denies any reality to the immaterial. What we have explained here is known as the hylomorphic[12] view of reality in Moderate Realism.[13]

Things do not exist because they have matter, but because they have an act of existence. Likewise, individual man is a compound of accidents that differentiate him from other men. All of his particular accidents make him an existing individual. Yet, his form of essence, his humanness, makes him what he is, i.e., a man. Thus, his essence must differ from his individuality.

What does all this have to do with teaching apologetics? The subject of apologetics claims to be able to prove the Christian faith. The educator of apologetics wants to teach an apologetics that is successful in proving the Christian faith. Both endeavors rely on and start from a knowable existing reality. Therefore, a suitable philosophy that explains reality must support both endeavors. Only moderate realism provides the proper philosophical background and explanation for understanding realty that clears the way for teaching and doing apologetics. Peter Kreeft explains,

12. All natural things change (i.e., accidentally and substantial change such as that which terminates their being) including human beings contain two principles of reality: matter (Gk. *hyle*) and form (Gk. *morphe*).

13. Contemporary Philosophers representing this approach include Etienne Gilson (1884–1978) and Joseph Owens (1908–2005).

> Many modern philosophers are suspicious and skeptical of the venerable and commonsense notion of things having real essences or natures and of our ability to know them. Aristotelian logic assumes the existence of essences and our ability to know them, for its basic units are terms, which express concepts, which express essence. But modern symbolic logic does not assume what philosophers call metaphysical realism (that essences are real), but implicitly assumes instead metaphysical undeniable (that essences are only *nomina*, names, human labels), since its basic units are not terms but propositions[14]

To further elaborate, if we take the view that there are no essences (i.e., Nominalism[15]) which denies any knowable essences outside or inside the mind, then there really can never be any knowable evidence sufficient to establish the fact that something exists or even that Jesus was seen by eyewitness alive after he died. Since these claims involve a knowable reality (i.e., essence) teaching apologetics under any other, philosophical metaphysic (e.g., Idealism, Materialism, or Nominalism) would be unsuccessful if not irrelevant.

NATURAL THEOLOGY

A central element of apologetics, in the classical tradition, is the ability to express and demonstrate according to human reason that God does exist and must exist in a certain way. Arguments for God's existence should be offered to prove that God exists. Hence, if an argument is valid and true then it stands as a proof for the existence of God. This is different than persuading someone that God exists. An argument may or may not do that for any number of reasons (i.e., psychological, moral, etc.). It is also important to realize that there are many ways, apart from formal rational argumentation, in which people come to believe in God. They may have been brought up in a family, culture, or religion that asserts a form of theism. They may have an insight into the way the world is, and concluded that there must be a God. However, this fact does not negate

---

14. Kreeft and Tacelli, *Handbook of Christian Apologetics*, 15.

15. Nominalism holds that universals are not real. Universals are categories or concepts that contain every item of a class. For a nominalist there is no such thing as treeness that is apart from the particular tree or thing. For a nominalist words become empty abstractions because there is no reality to the thing only a name. Universal ideas are not ontologically real. Two well-known nominalist are Duns Scotus (1266–1308) and William of Ockham (1280–1349).

the possibility of human reasoning concerning the existence of God. The many ways one may come to believe in God are not mutually exclusive.

Another important aspect of arguments for God, related to apologetics, concerns the difference between believing *that* God exists and believing *in* God. The difference is very important for the subject of apologetics and for the teacher and student. Failure to realize its significance can have devastating consequences for the spiritual life of a student. Apologetics concerns arguments *that* God exists and *that* Christianity is true. But this is very different then causing someone to believe *in* God or *in* Jesus Christ. Believing that something is true, involves the intellect. Believing *in* something involves the will. Apologetics is able to establish *that* Christianity is true, but it cannot make someone believe *in* Christ. God or even Christianity can easily become an object of pure intellectual curiosity for the apologetic student. But Christian education desires much more of the student. The student should become a follower of Jesus Christ. This involves love, obedience, commitment, and the work of the Holy Spirit in the life of the believer. Hence, there is a danger for the student and even the teacher of apologetics to become spiritually dull or impassionate about Christ; to view Him only as an object of study. A course in apologetics must engage the student in more than just knowledge about Christianity. It must try to engage and challenge the student spiritually as well as intellectually in a Christ-centered environment in hopes of facilitating spiritual growth and godliness.

Generally, arguments for the existence of God can be classified in one of four types: Cosmological (cosmos meaning world), Teleological (teleos meaning design), Axiological (axiom meaning judgment), and Ontological (ontos meaning being). The first three types of arguments reason from effect to cause and are called *a posteriori* the last one reasons from cause to effect and is called *a priori*. There is a reason to favor one of these approaches over the other. Etienne Gilson (1884–1978), a Thomistic philosopher, explains why, "In all cases, demonstrations proceed from that which is better known to that which is less well known. In the present case, we have practically no choice. The nature of God is less known to us than that of His effects. Consequently, all demonstrations of the existence of God must start from our knowledge of some of His effects."[16]

The cosmological argument comes in two forms (Figure 5.1). The first is called a horizontal form or originating cause and was championed

---

16. Gilson, "Can the Existence of God Still be Demonstrated?" 1.

by St. Bonaventure (1224–1274) and Islamic scholars in the Middle Ages who called their theology Kalām. A contemporary Christian author who has renewed interest in this argument is William Lane Craig.[17] This argument reasons that since there was a beginning to the universe there must be a Cause. The second form of the cosmological argument is called a vertical or continuing cause. A form of it was made by Thomas Aquinas. Contemporary apologist Norman L. Geisler has reevaluated and strengthened this argument.[18] It reasons that if contingent beings exist now, there must be a non-contingent (or eternal) being causing them to exist. As indicated earlier, the correct starting point for this kind of argument is existential undeniability, rather than a principle of *a priori* reason alone (see chapter 2).

TWO ASPECTS OF CREATION

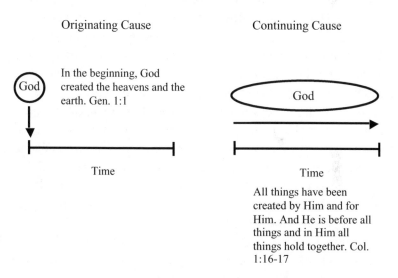

Originating Cause

Continuing Cause

In the beginning, God created the heavens and the earth. Gen. 1:1

Time

Time

All things have been created by Him and for Him. And He is before all things and in Him all things hold together. Col. 1:16-17

Figure 5.1 Vertical and Horizontal Cosmological Arguments Compared[19]

The teleological argument made famous by William Paley has recently seen renewed interest in the work of some scientists under the movement Intelligent Design.[20] Here it is reasoned that if intelligent

---

17. See Craig, *The Existence of God & the Beginning of the Universe* and Craig, *The Kalām Cosmological Argument.*

18. Geisler and Corduan, *Philosophy of Religion.*

19. Geisler and Brooks, *When Skeptics Ask*, 19. Used by Permission.

20. Behe, *Darwin's Black Box.*

design exists in the world, there must be an intelligent Designer of the world. The axiological or moral argument was made popular by C. S. Lewis in his *Mere Christianity*. If transcendent universal moral laws exist, then there must be a moral law Giver.

The ontological argument was brought to maturity in the writings of St. Anselm. But here we must remember that this argument is *a priori* and is a departure from the *a posteriori* approach. It reasons that necessary existence must be attributed to the most perfect being, because it is inconceivable for the greatest conceivable being not to have necessary existence. Most theists acknowledge that the ontological argument does have problems. Immanuel Kant's assessment observed that there is a difference in thinking about a ten dollar bill, and actually having one in your wallet. In short, this argument shows us that we must think of God in a necessary way, but it does not show us that God necessarily exists. However, Kant incorrectly went one step further and applied this critique to the other arguments for God's existence. He reasoned that the traditional arguments reduce to the invalid ontological argument. This is not the case; valid cosmological type arguments do not depend or reduce to the ontological. What they do, is *use* the ontological in a definition of God. Hence, there is an important role the ontological argument has when it is combined with other arguments such as the cosmological. Because it does tell us some important things about what God must be like, if indeed, God does exist, He must be a necessary being.

There are two important values to these arguments for an apologetics course.[21] First, it is important to our philosophy that we understand that such arguments are demonstrative. That is they do use valid human reason to demonstrate that God exists. A failure here will leave the apologetic student with no assurance that apologetics will be successful in ultimately proving that Christianity is true.

Second, an apologetics course must show how all these arguments relate to the God of Scripture. It may be clear that they conclude that God exists, but how do we know this God is the same God of the Bible? One way to do this is to combine all these arguments together, to discover what kind of God exists. For example, we learn from these arguments that God is all powerful, all good, eternal, infinite, and a

---

21. It is worth noting that there are other arguments for the existence of God that can be explored for educational purposes. See Kreeft and Tacelli, *Handbook of Christian Apologetics*, 48–88.

necessary being. When we turn to the Scriptures we see that the same God described by our philosophical argument must be the same God described in Scripture (Heb 1:2; Mal 3:6; 1 Kn 8:27; Ps 86:5; Heb 1:3). Since the God of our philosophy agrees with the God of the Bible, they must be identical. There can be only one Being that is all powerful, all-good, eternal, infinite, and necessary. A failure to make this connection will leave the student with no application of these arguments to serve as a foundation or prolegomena to disciplines such as theology and even biblical studies.

SCIENCE

Perhaps there is no wider known conflict then that which has historically raged between science and Christianity. It is not just the persistent conflict between evolutionists and creationists. While it may not be essential to the task of apologetics, the apologetics teacher will be asked to answer questions about the integration of the Bible, particularly Genesis, and modern Science? How old is the universe; the earth; and humans? How do the dinosaurs fit into Genesis and modern Science? Students, even before their secondary school years, are asking these questions. Admittedly, many Bible teachers tremble at the complexities of these questions and issues where even among Christian scholars there is little agreement. Yet, there are some important principles to understand that can clarify the subject of science and guide the process of teaching apologetics especially where they intersect.

We have already explained the first principle that recognizes that the conflict is not between what God created, a natural world and inspired scriptural words, but lies with human fallible understanding and investigation of these domains (see chapter 4). This distinction will go a long way in clarifying why sometimes there is a real conflict between scientists and theologians and at the same time admit that there is a certain solution or adequate reconciliation whether it is humanly discoverable or not.

A second principle concerns an important distinction to make between two kinds of science: Operation and origin.[22] Operation science concerns science that investigates that which is observable, repeatable, and hence testable in the natural world. The method of inquiry is the

---

22. Geisler and Anderson, *Origin Science*.

modern scientific method that formulates and tests a hypothesis. The result yields inductive conclusions based on probability. One example of operation science is the observable genetic changes within species due to environmental surroundings. This is observable in species today. The investigation as to why and how these changes occur is the proper domain of operation science. Origin science, on the other hand, investigates unobservable, singular, events that occurred in the past. Origin science may still involve elements of the scientific method, but it is never able to observe the original phenomena. Hence, it must approach its investigation similar to a detective and again only reach probable conclusions. For example, the origin of the universe and first life, are properly understood to be the domain of origin science since they are unrepeatable.

Failing to keep the results and process of these sciences distinct has contributed to the conflict between creation and evolution. The evolutionist has taken the conclusions of one method of science (microevolution) that investigates the operations of present day life forms that include changes within species, and applied them as a theory about the origin of past life forms (macroevolution). Yet there is no adequate mechanism to account for this kind of change.[23] The result is a supposed scientific theory (macroevolution) in conflict with special revelation (Gen 1).

Another important principle to consider is the very limitation of scientific knowledge itself. The conclusions and discoveries of science, while having considerable impact and impressive technical applications evident in our culture, is still inductive and at best highly probably in nature. Hence, some of the most accepted discoveries of science are still described as theories and only a few have made it to the higher status of law. A history of science clearly reveals the limitations, extensive revisions, and refinements that continue to be made to scientific understanding of our natural world.[24] Given this, the Christian should not fear science as ever being able to upset one's faith. A scientific theory or

23. Natural selection is put forth as this mechanism, however, this presupposes a replicating system and the only evidence for the biological component of this theory remains microevolution (genetic changes within species) which has never empirically been observed, tested, or adequately explained at the macro evolutionary level. See Bradley and Thaxton, "Information & the Origin of Life," in Moreland, *Creation Hypothesis*, 173–210.

24. See Brush, *The Limitations of Scientific Truth*.

understanding that seems, at present, to conflict with essential Christian belief, because of the nature of the subject, is always tentative.

As we have said earlier, there is no disagreement or error between general and special revelation because they have the same Creator (see chapter 4). But there are real disagreements and conflicts between science and theology. So it is valid to ask, in such cases of conflict, which discipline is to be given priority in an attempt to settle a disagreement. While we might be tempted to put the Bible first, it should be kept in mind that human interpretation of the infallible word is subject to man's fallible understanding. This is also true for science. As Norman Geisler insightfully suggests, "The interaction between biblical studies and other disciplines should always be a two-way street. No one provides a monologue for the other; all engage in continual dialogue. Although the Bible is infallible in whatever it addresses, it does not speak to every issue. Furthermore, . . . while the Bible is infallible, our interpretation of it is not. Thus, those in biblical studies must listen to as well as speak to the other disciplines. Only in this way can a complete and correct systematic world view be constructed."[25] Priority then should go to the interpretation or understanding that is more clear and certain, while understanding that revisions may have to be made when new evidence in either science or theology becomes available.

For example, consider some clearly false interpretations of the Bible that have historically been held by some. In Joshua 1:15 it states that the sun rises (moves around the earth). Yet, this need not imply, as some have understood it, that the sun must move around the earth. Instead, this is observational or phenomenal language frequently used even today since it describes what is observed and not what is actually the case. There are also some clear false understandings in science to consider. The naturalistic theory of evolution, for example, asserts that all the different variety of living organisms are the result of macro evolutionary change. However, the Bible clearly asserts that each was created after its kind and humans are in the image of God (Gen 1:21; 27). One scientific problem is that there is no adequate mechanism put forth to account for such change, and there is a clear understanding of the scriptural statements and meaning. Hence, priority must be given to Scripture because of its clearer teaching.

---

25. Geisler, *Introduction and Bible*, 79

It is also worth noting that there are other areas where we currently may not have enough evidence or grasp of the issue from either a scientific or theological position. In such cases we may not be able to speak with certainty on questions related to nature and Scripture. One example of this may be the length of time involved in God's creation. Theologians disagree with each other on the specific interpretation of the word "day" in Genesis chapter 1.

These principles understood in the context of teaching apologetics as a subject can be used to help clarify many areas of real and perceived conflict between science and theology. Apologetics can and should explore these areas with confidence since God is the infallible creator.

HISTORY

After the first step of classical apologetics, which mostly involves philosophy and natural theology, the second step completely relies on the assertion that some things in history are knowable and hence provable. History is the study of the past to discover what has taken place. Historiography is the task of the historian by which he constructs a written text about the past based on evidence. The study of the past is an essential aspect of apologetics. The Bible claims God has intervened in human history. If this is undiscoverable or unknowable, then there is no way to discover truth about God's activities or miraculous interventions in the past. Even if the knowability of history is possible, we must still use proper methods for discovering it.

Our question regarding the knowability of history is really the same battle between relativism and objectivity. The person who asserts, "Historical statements or claims about the past are not objectively true or knowable." Either the statement is true or it is false. If it is true then it is a historical statement that claims to be objective and knowable. Hence it is self-defeating. If it is false, then historical statements that are objective and knowable are possible. Since we have already established that relativism is false (see page 68f.), it is possible to assert that if a historical statement is verifiable, according to appropriate historical methods, then it is true (i.e., corresponds to reality).

Some may object by insisting that a historian, as any interpreter, brings their presuppositions and cultural influence to the task of historiography. If so it would seem that they are unable to be completely objective in their task. However, all discovery of truth, historical included, involves individual presuppositions and cultural influence. If this is the case then the issue is not whether objectivity in history is possible, but rather whose presuppositions are correct. There must be an objective ground for all statements, historical or otherwise, because, as we have shown (see page 28f.), there are universal principles that apply to everyone, including the historian. Disagreement over historical statements, presuppositions, or cultural influence should not give way to relativism.

There are some important things that make the knowability of history more likely. First, the correct world view is theistic. Since there is an absolute Mind that knows everything (past, present, and future) from eternity, history really becomes His-story. We are not saying that a historian with a different world view (e.g., Atheistic) is unable to arrive at any historical truth. However, since theism is the true world view, only a theistic historian has what is necessary in their world view to properly discover and classify events that have taken place in the past. For example, if one were to discover historical evidence for a miracle that occurred in the past. Only the theistic historian is able to properly classify and explain such an event. The atheistic historian has no way to incorporate a theistic miracle into their understanding of history. They are forced, because of their world view, to classify, regardless of the evidence, such an event in natural terms such as a myth, hoax, or an anomaly yet to be explained. Second, as was indicated earlier, the philosophy, skill, expertise, and the well roundedness of the historian are extremely important. The truthfulness of the historical work, as Jacques Maritain states, "will be in proportion to the human richness of the historian."[26] It is when the individual historian is able to bring together the inductive facts of history with the "rational light of philosophical analysis"[27] that history is objective.

Third, it is important to realize the nature of history as a subject of investigation. Philosopher Mortimer J. Adler helps us in this endeavor by saying, "On the one hand, we have self-evident truths that have certitude and incorrigibility; and we also have truths that are still subject to doubt but that are supported by evidence and reason to a degree that puts them beyond reasonable doubt or at least give them predominance over contrary views. All else is mere opinion—with no claim to being knowledge or having any hold on truth. . . . There is no question that

26. Maritain, *On The Philosophy of History*, 7–8.
27. Ibid., 11.

the findings and conclusions of historical research are knowledge in this sense."[28] While it is admitted that perfect absolute objectivity is only possible for an infinite mind, (i.e., God) a theistic world view does provide the proper framework for the construction of a limited (i.e., open to revision) objective construction of the past.

EDUCATION

A philosophy of education is described as "the attempt to bring the insights and methods of philosophy to bear on the educational enterprise."[29] To do this we define the subject of education, describe philosophical positions in education, and discuss insights to the teaching-learning process.

Almost all of ones experiences in life result in some form or aspect of learning. John A. Laska helps narrow the focus of education to "the deliberate attempt by the learner or by someone else to *control* (or *guide*, or *direct*, or *influence*, or *manage*) a learning situation in order to bring about the attainment of a desired *learning outcome (goal)*."[30] Hence, education should be distinguished from the broader idea of *learning* that one experiences in life. The formal concept of *schooling* is also relevant. Individuals, today, usually go through a series of formal steps of progression from pre, middle, and secondary schooling. Some decide to go further into undergraduate, graduate, and other adult types of schooling (e.g., vocational training). Learning and education may take place in or outside the formal notion of school. Admittedly, for most people, the majority of learning and education may take place outside of schooling (Figure 5.2).[31] Learning involves knowing things that usually does not involve much effort for the simple reason that the intellect cannot help but perform its natural function. But educational instruction is to enable or cause a person to learn. What we teach them in school, although it may be a small part of their knowledge, imposing symbols in place of things, as Etienne Gilson remarks, "There is no natural relation between the letters of the alphabet and the sounds they are suppose to represent, nor between the words and the things they point out . . ."[32] This is also

---

28. Adler, *Ten Philosophical Mistakes*, 100–101.

29. Peterson, *Philosophy of Education*, 17.

30. Laska, *Schooling and Education*, 6.

31. Adapted from Knight, *Philosophy & Education*, 12.

32. Gilson, *The Eminence of Teaching*, 23.

the case for other subjects such as writing and arithmetic and the reason a teacher is necessary. The philosophy of education in view here is the narrower aspect of educational instruction in schooling that at least attempts to be controlled in view of desired outcomes in a formal setting.

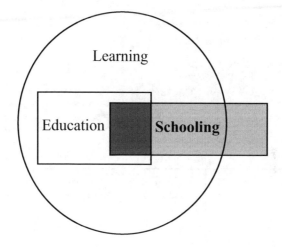

Figure 5.2 Relationship of Schooling-Education-Learning

The relationship between philosophy and educational philosophies is not always clear and agreed upon.[33] Depending on its proponent, an educational theory may be developed from within, outside, or in ignorance of the philosophical position of Moderate Realism which was discussed earlier (see page 73ff.). Educational theories can historically be divided into classical and contemporary. The classical theories included Idealism, Realism,[34] Pragmatism, and Existentialism. The first two (Idealism and Realism) are usually considered authoritarian views and favors what is termed convergent thinking. They are authoritarian and convergent because they believe there is a body of knowledge and skills of the mind (Idealism) or world (Realism) that a student should

33. One study done on educational textbooks revealed disagreement as to which philosophy should be attributed to a philosopher. For example, Immanuel Kant was claimed by Idealists, Realists, and Pragmatism for holding their educational theory. See Clabauch and Rozycki, *Understanding Schools*, 565–71. A good comparison of the three major classical educational philosophies is Frankena, *Three Historical Philosophies of Education*.

34. The educational theory of realism should not be confused with the philosophical position of Moderate Realism discussed earlier.

be brought inline with (i.e., mastered) to function properly. The latter (Pragmatism and Existentialism) are non-authoritarian and divergent in thinking. Here, there is a belief that the body of knowledge and skills needed is the result of social experience (Pragmatism) or personal choice (Existentialism) to become a functioning member of society. Hence, there is no fixed body of knowledge or skills in view that must always be taught or mastered (Table 5.1).

	Authoritarian Views (Convergent Thinking)		Non-authoritarian views (Divergent Thinking)	
	Idealism	Realism	Pragmatism	Existentialism
Subject	of the mind	of the world (science)	of social experience	of personal choice
Teaching	for ideas	for information and skills	for problem solving	for societal context

Table 5.1 Authoritarian and Non-authoritarian Philosophies Compared

Furthermore, from these classical educational philosophies at least five major contemporary theories of education have emerged: Perennialism, Essentialism, Behaviorism, Progressivism, and Reconstructionism. Although these views may share some of the same principles, the first three favor the authoritarian philosophies and the last two favor the non-authoritarian view. Perennialism (Mortimer Adler), so named because of its belief that knowledge is everlasting, focuses on the great ideas, works of literature, and traditional disciplines of the humanities, mathematics, science, and the arts. Essentialism (William C. Bagley) holds to a common core of information and skills needed for a person to function in society. But the core is understood as changing due to the changing nature of society. Behaviorism (B. F. Skinner) is a psychological approach to education that believes the environment determines behavior and the school should shape the environment to achieve observable behaviors. Progressivism (John Dewey) favors the scientific method and human experience as a basis for knowledge. The emphasis is on *how* to think as opposed to *what* to think. Reconstructionism (Theodore Barmeld) is concerned with restructuring schools to teach students to critically evaluate and explore controversial issues. The goal is usually to produce societal change.

Contemporary theories of education often do not make arguments or express a comprehensive view of reality. They do, however, make assumptions about reality which can often be opposed to the Christian world view. Caution and discretion must be used by the Christian educator in adapting beliefs and practices in education from a classical or contemporary philosophy. However, this is not to exclude that some valid observations regarding teaching and learning are not to be found or incorporated into an apologetics education program from other philosophies. Such theories or practices from other philosophies of education may nonetheless contain valid observations about human education and its process that fall under the realm of general revelation. For example, apologetics, as a subject of study, leans toward an Authoritarian or convergent thinking approach. In agreement with convergent thinking, apologetics is a body of knowledge of which the student should understand the meaning. Students must learn answers to apologetic questions and issues: more than that they must learn the body of knowledge used in defending the Christian faith. Yet, there are aspects of other educational theories that can play a role in apologetic education. Ideas and skills should be developed in discerning apologetic issues and tactfully presenting answers. Gleaning from the emphasis of divergent thinking, apologetics can involve problem solving in which the student should be given experiences that help them identify apologetic problems and propose solutions. There is also an element of desiring the student to contribute to social change within our society by using and developing apologetics. Hence, there are likely to be contemporary societal issues or questions that should play a prominent role in a CAE program. So it is certainly possible to combine aspects of various educational theories, without making Christian education become dominated by any one major educational theory in an unhealthy sense.

All of this can be done in the context of a Christian world view. The Christian educator may combine aspects of various educational theories if they are not in conflict with revealed truth in special or general revelation. One must, however, keep in mind the limitations and revisable nature of educational theory and practice. The teacher of apologetics must be aware of the possible subtle influences of non-Christian world views dictating ideas and practices in education clearly in conflict with revelation.

It is important to recognize the level of the students who will receive apologetic education. There is a distinction between educating children and adults, which is formally known as pedagogy (children) and andragogy (adults).[35] Not realizing this important distinction is perhaps one of the biggest pitfalls a first year teacher will face in a secondary school apologetics class. In most cases, the teacher is highly motivated as an adult to learn the subject and they have successfully taught the subject to adults in the church. In their first attempt at taking the subject to teenagers they find that all their best efforts seem to fall on an uninterested and unmotivated student. Why is the adult learner so highly self-motivated to learn apologetics but the teenager is not? While there are still similarities between andragogy and pedagogy learning, the major difference associated with pedagogy include: 1) Students depend more on the teacher for guidance; 2) the student has less experience and background regarding the subject; 3) the student needs to internalize their need for the subject, 4) the student needs more help in understanding the subjects application to life; and 5) the student needs more motivation and incentive to learn the material.

The teaching-learning process, as recognized by most educators, includes three domains commonly referred to as *cognitive, affective,* and *psychomotor*.[36] Cognitive consists of gaining knowledge and new insights. Cognitive learning is put into practice by having students engage in watching, listening, and thinking skills. Affective consists of developing attitudes and feelings. This form of learning will come through personal experiences with people, things, and ideas. Psychomotor is the development of new skills. It is accomplished when the student is engaged in activity or "learning by doing." Learning is most successful when all three of these domains are interwoven in the student's experience. Effective teaching is accomplished by causing students to be improved through the acquisition of organized knowledge, the development of intellectual skills, and the enlargement of understanding, insight, and appreciation.

Lawrence Richards and Gary Breadfeldt have identified levels of learning. The first concerns the ability to repeat or recognize information. It is the most basic level, but is ultimately insufficient. The next level, restatement, concerns the ability to express or relate concepts to an overall system or world view. This is more desirable, but only the

35. Knowles, *The Adult Learner.*

36. Bloom, et al. *Taxonomy of Educational Objectives.*

last level is the most desirable for education. This includes the ability to relate truth to life and realize its implication and application in the experience of everyday life. All of this can be accomplished through three principles: *motivation, relevance,* and *activity.*[37] Motivation is creating a desire in the students to want to learn, which is directly related to the student's interests and needs. Relevance shows the learner how the information relates to them personally. Activity is the putting into practice what is learned whether it be physical, mental, or emotional. Richards states, "When the student can see relationship between the concepts he or she has learned in class and everyday life, the possibility of the student actually making the transfer of learning to life is enhanced."[38]

Education is best achieved when goals or objectives are stated which are measurable and specific. Robert F. Mager has described an objective as "useful to the extent that it conveys to others a picture of what a successful learner will be like that is identical to the picture the objective-writer had in mind."[39] Objectives are best when the statements are detailed and the words used are precise. We should at least be able to state specifically what the learner should be able to do. Some words are vague and hard to measure. Consider the following objectives:

1. The student should *know* apologetic terms.

2. The student should *internalize* self-evident truths.

3. The student should *understand* self-referential statements.

These are objectives but the verb describing what the learner should be able to do is too vague and not measurable. They could be restated as follows:

1. The student should *define* Christian apologetic terms.

2. The student should *state* self-evident truths.

3. The student should *identify* self-referential statements.

These objectives are more specific and measurable. For example, we can now measure the child's ability by asking them to define, state, or identify. It is possible, however, to be even more descriptive and spe-

---

37. Zuck, *The Holy Spirit in Your Teaching,* 156–65.

38. Richards and Bredfeldt, *Creative Bible Teaching,* 126.

39. Mager, *Preparing Instructional Objectives,* 19.

cific, and the apologetic teacher is encouraged to do so if necessary. For example,

1. When given a test at the end of unit 1-A the student should write a correct *definition* of Christian apologetic terms.

2. When given a test at the end of unit 1-A the student should write a correct *statement* that expresses a self-evident truth.

3. When given a test at the end of unit 1-A the student should correctly *identify* a self-referential statement.

In these objectives, we have identified an actual context, a test, in which the student will perform the stated objective. The context does not always have to be a written test, for example, it may be in a group, role playing, or actual ministry setting that involves apologetic oral questions and answers.

Goals and objectives can be stated for the three domains of cognitive, affective, and psychomotor. They should be measurable so that the teacher and student can discover if the objective has been achieved. They should be specific, as opposed to general, so that both the teacher and student are clear on what is expected to achieve the objective. For example, the objective that says, "At the end of this lesson the student will *know* arguments for the existence of God," is too vague to inform the teacher or student as to what he or she should do to measure its outcome. Instead, the more specific objective should state: "At the end of this lesson the student will *write* an argument for the existence of God." This objective describes the kind of skill or task needed to measure the objective. Objectives, in order to achieve measurability, may have to be given a context in which they are to be achieved. For example, it might say, "Given a test question, the student will write an argument for the existence of God." Writing specific objectives for the three domains of learning can clarify expectations and help ensure learning is taking place.

General revelation is the realm of all human knowledge acquired apart from special revelation. The Christian educator is on sound biblical ground for acquiring knowledge and studying subjects in this realm to support the teaching of apologetics. Such knowledge and investigation should be appropriate to the nature of the subject and involve the use of appropriate means, operations, and procedures. Only this will ensure a realistic and teachable apologetic for Christianity. In the next chapter we turn to develop an understanding of some additional subjects that guide us to special revelation which will continue our development of an educational philosophy for apologetics.

QUESTIONS TO ANSWER

1. Describe the role moderate realism plays in developing a philosophy for teaching apologetics.

2. Describe what you consider to be the best argument for the existence of God in teaching apologetics.

3. Develop a philosophy for teaching apologetics that integrates an understanding of the teaching-learning-process.

SELECT READINGS

Frederic R. Howe, *Challenge and Response.* Chapter 7–8, 10.

Frederick D. Wilhelmsen, *Man's Knowledge of Reality.*

Etienne Gilson, "Can the Existence of God Still be Demonstrated?" and "The Eminence of Teaching"

6

Toward a Philosophy of Christian Education
for Apologetics: Special Revelation

OBJECTIVES

Discern the difference between the orthodox view of biblical inspiration and other views.

Integrate biblical principles of education into a philosophy for teaching apologetics.

A S EXPLAINED IN THE previous chapter special revelation is the sphere or realm of supernatural truth that is discovered only by investigating the written text of Scripture. God inspired (2 Tim 3:16–17; 2 Pet 1:20–1) the writers of Scripture to write an inerrant and authoritative text that reveals truth about God and creation which is not discoverable through human investigation of general revelation. To further our progress in developing a philosophy of apologetic education we will consider the theological subjects of biblical inspiration, hermeneutics, the Holy Spirit, and finally Christian education.

BIBLICAL INSPIRATION

There are four major views of inspiration. The first is the traditional orthodox or evangelical understanding that asserts that the Bible *is* the word of God.[1] The Liberal or Modern understanding believes the Bible *contains* the word of God (Harold DeWolf).[2] The Neo-Orthodox view

---

1. One contemporary representation of this view can be found in the Chicago Statement on Scripture (1978) formulated by the International Council on Biblical Inerrancy (ICBI), see Geisler and Nix, *A General Introduction to the Bible*, 181–85.

2. DeWolf, *The Case for Theology in Liberal Perspective*.

says the Bible *becomes* the word of God (Karl Barth).[3] Finally, the most recent view is the Neo-Evangelical which believes intentions or concepts contain the word of God (G. C. Berkouwer).[4] The orthodox or evangelical view is claimed by Scripture itself and defendable on philosophical and historical grounds.[5] If inspiration does not apply to the text of Scripture then we have no certain means of arriving at an objective understanding. Furthermore, if inspiration allows for any aspect of scientific or historical error then the nature of God, who inspired the human author, is brought into question. Hence, only an approach that properly recognizes the Bible as God-breathed and inerrant in the original writings can properly serve as a foundation for Christian education.

Norman Geisler in his *Systematic Theology* defines inspiration as "the supernatural operation of the Holy Spirit, who through the different personalities and literary styles of the chosen human authors invested the very words of the original books of the Holy Scripture, alone and in their entirety, as the very Word of God without error in all that they teach or imply (including history and science), and the Bible is thereby the infallible rule and final authority for faith and practice of all believers."[6]

Special revelation also means that there are no personal revelations given to individuals today. This view asserts that the only special revelation that exists today is what is contained in canonical Scriptures. It is for all believers. There is no more special revelation, either normative or private, to be given. Thus, the Scriptures are the sole source for personal guidance, direction, and decision making concerning the will of God. Areas that fall outside the realm of scriptural guidance are left to the free decision of the believer. That is not to say, however, that wisdom cannot be sought from God (Jam 1:5) to help especially in difficult situations. Such wisdom is available from various sources, but circumstances or inner impressions should not be interpreted as personal signs from God. Rather, a proper role of circumstance is to understand them as opportunities by which we have been given the freedom and responsibility to make wise decisions in accordance with God's word.[7] This point

3. Barth, *Church Dogmatics*, vol. 1, *The Doctrine of the Word of God*.

4. Berkouwer, *Holy Scripture*.

5. See Geisler, *General Introduction*, part 1.

6. Geisler, *Introduction Bible*, 241.

7. For a defense and explanation of this view see Friesen and Maxson, *Decision Making and the Will of God*.

may produce some controversy for the teacher of apologetics since many within the evangelical church do believe that God gives personal revelation or special guidance today. However, this should be objected to on the basis that God's revelation, even in personal matters, must be inerrant and contain the full level of inspiration as previous written revelation. If not, then it is not from God. The apologetic teacher is also aware of the numerous cults and groups that claim direct revelation from God and additional written texts on par with the Bible. An apologists that does not limit scriptural revelation to the canonical texts of the Bible, leaves the door open for anyone to claim new revelation and the unending task of having to take such claims seriously until an examination proves to be unorthodox according to Scripture.

BIBLICAL INTERPRETATION

A proper apologetic demands that there be a correct methodology of interpretation. After all, we cannot conduct a class on defending the Christian faith; if we can not properly interpret it we will make the Bible mean anything we want it to. The subject of study that gives us principles to interpret a text is known as hermeneutics, which involves the use of the historical-grammatical method of interpretation. Simply put, this means that to understand properly any text the historical and grammatical sense must be understood. But even when this method is properly applied, can the student be sure that an interpretation is objective?

In interpretation, there is one thing universally acknowledged: When a reader comes to any given text they come with presuppositions or preunderstanding. These include the point of view, background, assumptions and overall world view of the interpreter. Likewise, it is agreed that an interpreter cannot completely separate himself or herself from their presuppositions. There is no such thing as an interpreter completely devoid of presuppositions. This has caused many to conclude that an objective interpretation is not possible. Hence, with so many different interpretations there is no way to tell whose interpretation is finally correct.

Such a view is clearly grounded in a relativistic understanding of truth. But as we have shown relativism as applied to truth is self-defeating (see page 68ff). Yet, a subjective theory of interpretation is claiming, "There is no objective interpretation." If the statement is true, then it must apply to every interpretation including any interpretation of this very statement. But this would seem to entail that there is some objective or universal truth or principle of interpretation since it is applicable to all interpretations. In other words, should we interpret the statement, "There is no objective interpretation" subjectively or objectively? If objectively then it is false. If subjectively then it is not applicable to all interpretations and the door is open to the possibility of objectivity.

As Dr. Thomas A. Howe explains, "The fact of the matter is, objectivity is not only possible, but it is also unavoidable. Even the critics of objectivity think that you, as a reader, can objectively understand their objections to objectivity. The reason it is important to establish that objectivity is possible is that without it there could be no communication. There would be no way to know whether we had correctly understood what was said or whether our preunderstanding had entirely distorted it."[8] There is no doubt that some of our preunderstanding or perspective is unique to us, based on our experience, culture, world view, etc. It is interesting that everyone seems to acknowledge that a reader comes to a text with presuppositions and is not able to separate completely from these. Even one who says, "I will come to the text objectively," is bringing this presupposition to the text. But it is in these acknowledgements that we are able to see an example of objectivity. Regardless of background, presuppositions, or world view everyone has acknowledged the presence of a readers presuppositions. Hence, there is something common and objective about this very claim that demonstrates the possibility of objectivity. Objectivity is possible because there are principles of communication that are universal. Because of this, it is possible to use principles of interpretation to adjudicate conflicting interpretations. Another important aspect of reality is that there exists an absolute Mind that knows everything. Hence, there is an absolute perspective by which objectivity may be discovered and known. Since there is an eternal absolute understanding their may exist by analogy finite minds that may have adequate finite objectivity in interpretation.

Since, the results of interpretation can be objective there must be only one correct interpretation of any given text. While there can be multiple applications of a specific text(s), there can be only one meaning for a text. While disagreements may exist over certain interpretations, the possibility of having and expressing an objective interpretation is always possible. Two observations support this conclusion. First, argu-

8. Howe, "Practical Hermeneutics," 26–27.

ments against objectivity are self-defeating. The statement "no interpretation can be objective" either result in an objective interpretation in which case it is wrong, or it has some bias associated with it. Another way to consider the problem is if everyone expresses a bias in their interpretation, then there still must be objectivity because everyone does this (i.e., expresses a bias). The dilemma is not whether or not there is objectivity. But whose "bias" or presupposition is correct which would reveal their interpretation to be the objective one.

The second reason concerns a moderate realist metaphysic, which understands meaning as existing in the text, and can come to exist in the mind of the reader (see page 73ff). This is described in two principles of form and matter discussed earlier. The process of knowing takes place when the form, or meaning in the case of sensible text in reality, actually enters the knowing subject's mind. That is, the thing known actually comes to exist in the mind of the perceiver. Hence, the meaning of words, in so far as they form units of meaning (i.e., sentences), are truly known by the knower as it occurs in itself.[9]

This philosophical background while clearly legitimizing scriptural interpretation will not eliminate the arising of different and sometimes conflicting interpretations in a course on apologetics. But it should give solid ground to the student and teacher to work towards a correct interpretation by knowing that such is indeed humanly possible.

THE HOLY SPIRIT AND APOLOGETICS EDUCATION

Understanding who the Holy Spirit is and what He does is essential to developing a balanced educational apologetics program. We have already acknowledged the numerous imperatives and exhortations in Scripture concerning the need for apologetics (chapter 1). It is therefore important to acknowledge the internal work of the Holy Spirit and the limitations of human apologetics. After all we have said about the importance of apologetics, it is important to acknowledge a person does not have to have apologetics to come to faith in Jesus Christ as their savior. That is to say, apologetics, as important as it is and may be so more today than at any other time in history, is not necessary for faith. But the gospel and internal work of the Holy Spirit, convicting a person of their sin is neces-

---

9. For an extensive review and defense of this point see Howe, *Objectivity in Biblical Interpretation*.

sary. However, if the person before or even after their conversion, wants to know that what they believe is the truth; then, they must use apologetics. If apologetics is not used for this verification, then their personal experience, whatever it may be is no more valid then the experience of a person who is converted to a non-Christian religion such as Hinduism or a cult such as Mormonism.

From the pages of Scripture, we discover that the Holy Spirit works on the heart of the unbeliever (Jn 16:8) and in the life of the believer (1 Cor 2:13, 14). The Holy Spirit specifically convicts the unbeliever of their sinful condition. This internal persuasion or conviction should not be confused with the task of apologetics. Apologetics, properly done, provides reasons and evidence *that* shows Christianity to be true. But the Holy Spirit, alone, provides the persuasion to believe *in* Jesus Christ. Belief *in* Jesus needs no defense or reason. It is a free act of the will. Belief *that* Christianity is true, however, is a position of the mind or intellect in which one is or can be persuaded based on reason and evidence concerning the truth of the Christian faith. A balanced educational apologetics program must acknowledge and operate in complete awareness of these two tasks. Both are often in operation together.

The Holy Spirit is also involved in the teaching-learning process through the teacher and student who must properly be related to each other through Jesus Christ. For learning that is superintended by the Spirit, both the teacher and student must have confessed sin in their life to God (1 Jn 1:9). It is only then that the Spirit can properly be said, to have filled or empowered the teacher and student. The Holy Spirit, in education, is a giver and helper. He is a giver to the teacher of the spiritual gift of teaching regardless of the subjects taught.[10] The teacher must discover and exercise or develop this giftedness. Such a gift does not excuse the teacher from study and preparation or even understanding the educational process, but it does give the teacher guidance, power, illumination, and insight that can only come from the Holy Spirit working through the yielded and obedient life of a teacher engaged in the process.[11]

10. Although all believers are given at least one spiritual gift (1 Cor 12:11), it may not be necessary for a believer to be given the spiritual gift of teaching to teach apologetics, since all believers and church leaders are admonished to teach (Col 3:16; 1 Tim 3:2; 2 Tim 2:24).

11. Some have suggested that apologetics may be a spiritual gift attached to evangelism as in Eph 4:11. While there is a diversity of gifts (1 Cor 12:4) and no list in the

Since students have minds or intellects created by God they do not need the Sprits help to think or understand. What the student does need help with, via the Holy Spirit, is taking what they do know and applying it to their personal lives and ministry. This is properly known as the illuminating work of the Holy Spirit. It is here that the Holy Spirit influences us to use and apply truth to our lives and thinking so we can recognize opportunities to use it. Apologetics, being the subject that supplies the reason why Christianity is true, can be used in the life of the student via the Holy Spirit's work. Hence, apologetics becomes a tool or handmaid used by the Sprit in ministry and other life experiences that the student would normally be doing. But unlike the uneducated believer, the spiritual student is able, by the guidance and providential leading in the power of the Holy Spirit, to recognize and perform apologetics in various circumstances to meet needs and help accomplish the Sprits work.

CHRISTIAN EDUCATION

It is worthwhile to note the foundation of all Christian education. Jesus Christ gave an imperative to his followers, which became the Church, that as they went they were to make disciples baptizing and teaching them to observe all that He commanded (Matt 28:18–20). For children, at the secondary school level, responsibility for this instruction is clearly in the home. The family relies on a love commitment between the husband and wife (Gen 2:24; Matt 19:1–6). This is where spiritual development takes place. Deuteronomy 6:4–9 explains that instruction from God's word should be a regular (i.e., daily) part of family life. Frank Stanger in his book *Spiritual Formation in the Local Church* gives a succinct definition of what this is: "The intentional systematic process of growing into the image of Christ through obedience to the Scriptures by the power of the Holy Spirit in our total personality."[12] Parents should be involved in intentional and systematic planning to instruct their children. This is not to diminish the role of God's spirit or to say there should be no times of informal spiritual formation. Much of spiritual formation is probably learned from informal life experiences. However, it is the parents' responsibility to plan for and provide the spiritual instruction. The goal

---

New Testament should be taken as comprehensive, apologetics is not specifically listed as a gift.

12. Stanger, *Spiritual Formation in the Local Church*, 17

of spiritual instruction is to be conformed, by the power of God, to the image of His Son. This is the goal of building a relationship with Jesus Christ. This is a life long process that will not see complete fulfillment until Christ comes. All of this must be done in a context that acknowledges the Scriptures are the word of God and that it is God's work in the individual through the Holy Spirit (Phil 1:6). Hence, the center of Christian education is in the home and resides with the parents. This is the biblical model. All other means of Christian education whether they are in the Church or institutional Christian School should be a handmaid to the primary role of Christian education in the home.

While there are many things to be discovered in the pages of Scripture concerning Christian education that are not discoverable through general revelation, we will note just a few important things to consider regarding a Christian philosophy. First, God is triune consisting of one divine nature and three persons: Father, Son, and Holy Spirit. God is one self-existing, eternal, and infinite being. He is one divine nature (what he is) with three persons (who's or separate identities). Each is significant and described as having distinct roles in education. Jesus Christ is the goal of Christian living. His likeness is what the Christian should seek (Eph 4:15, 24; Phil 3:10; Rom 8:29; Col 1:28). This is accomplished only through cooperation with the power and inward work of the Holy Spirit (Rom 12:2; Gal 5:15). All of this is to bring honor and glory to the Father (Matt 5:16; 1 Pet 4:11).

Second, there are several important things to acknowledge about humans. All people are created in the image of God (Gen 1:27; Jas 3:9). This image however, is defaced by original and personal sin. This sinful nature affects the condition of every human by birth which results in depraved moral and physical condition culminating in spiritual and physical separation from God (i.e., death). The world, as a result, is in darkness (2 Cor 4:3–4), error (John 8:23), and evil (Rom 5:12; 1 John 2:16–17). There is nothing humans can do individually or collectively to save themselves from death. Salvation from such a condition can only be provided by their Creator. This salvation from a sinful nature is provided by the substitutionary death and bodily resurrection of Jesus Christ, the Son of God (Luke 24:38–39; 1 Cor 15:1–6). As a result humans can be renewed in God's image (Col 3:10) and can be taught by the Holy Spirit (1 Cor 2:13–14). They are capable of understanding God's truth and sharing His love (2 Cor 2:13–14).

Third, Christian education should always be done in an environment that is based on the Bible, centered on Christ (2 Cor 10:5), and honors God (1 Cor 10:31). The teacher should endeavor to know the truth (whether it be found in general or special revelation) and the contemporary world which he or she lives (1 Chr 12:32; Phil 2:14–15). These realms of knowledge should be taught to students who should also be instructed in how to think correctly and live righteously (Deut 6:4–9; Mark 12:29–31). Christian education should be done in an environment in which both teacher and student relate properly to God and one another through the Holy Spirit, in view of Jesus Christ's imminent return (Acts 1:7–8; 1 Thess 4:13–18).

Fourth, there are some principles relevant to the education process itself. A Christian education program should include outcome-based objectives that cover the spiritual realm (as opposed to just cognitive, affective, and psychomotor) of a student's life. These outcomes may not be subject specific (i.e., for math or science), but they should be stated expectations that cover an expected level of spirituality based on the age level of the student. A Christian education program should discover truth through special revelation (2 Tim 3:16–17). This truth should be transmitted and disseminate to students in a manner that *causes* them to learn (Deut 4:1; 5:1).

Finally, the Christian educator is responsible for defending the truth God has revealed (1 Pet 3:15; John 13:34–5). Apologetics is a necessary task and requires complete understanding by leaders within the church. Titus 1:7–9 states, "For the overseer must be . . . holding fast the faithful word which is in accordance with the teaching, so that he will be able both to exhort in sound doctrine and to refute those who contradict." As already indicated, the Scriptures contain numerous exhortations calling upon the believer to defend the Christian faith and gospel (chapter 1). One should expect nothing less from a Christian educator to include such instruction in their curriculum. And, as already argued, the best place to begin doing that is through teaching apologetics as a distinct subject of study at the secondary level (chapter 3).

CHRISTIAN APOLOGETICS EDUCATION

It is an important part of a philosophy to distinguish educational apologetics from other disciplines and give it a definition for the purpose of Christian education. Christian apologetics education should provide students with the opportunity to understand why the Christian world view alone is true. Therefore, in the context of a Christian education we may propose a definition as follows:

A Christ-centered, Bible-based and activity-oriented educational program for all students to learn how to communicate, defend, use and assess ideas and arguments that defends and advances the Christian faith.

By Christ-centered, it is meant that the instructional time is oriented around the person of Jesus Christ. His presence is acknowledged and His moral instruction, as contained in the Scripture, serves as the guide for behavior. By Bible-based it is meant that there is a biblical justification for the class being taught. As we have shown there are biblical imperatives to do apologetics that apply to all Christians, and there is a contemporary need for it to be done at the secondary level. Hence, there is a biblical justification for Christian education. By activity-oriented, it is meant that the class includes activities that reinforce concepts taught. The student should put into use, by communicating in real or imagined role-playing scenarios the concepts, arguments, and information taught in the class. Such an education is for every student, in the sense that every Christian is expected to be prepared to give an answer to anyone that asks (1 Pet 3:15). The purpose of the class is to equip the student to defend the Christian faith with the ultimate goal of advancing the cause of Christ.

General and special revelation should be used to develop and inform the Christian educational enterprise. Hence, an educational philosophy that counters or ignores conclusions from general and special revelation must be rejected. Yet, conclusions or insights from philosophers of education that agree, or are compatible with, general and special revelation should be integrated into a Christian philosophy of education. Hence, this philosophy can support the inclusion of apologetics as a subject of study. This does not, however, answer the questions of what should be in the curriculum. This we will cover in the next chapter.

QUESTIONS TO ANSWER

1. Describe and contrast the different views of biblical inspiration.

2. What role does objectivity in hermeneutics play in the teaching of apologetics?

3. Develop a philosophy for teaching apologetics that incorporates biblical principles of Christian education.

SELECT READINGS

Norman L. Geisler, *General Introduction to the Bible.* Part 1.

Thomas A. Howe, *Objectivity in Biblical Interpretation.*

Robert E. Clark, *Christian Education: Foundations for the Future.*

7

A Curriculum Model
for Christian Apologetics Education

OBJECTIVES

Recognize the foundational role apologetics plays in the curriculum.

Elucidate the curriculum model for apologetics.

Examine a text book for use in a secondary level apologetics class according to the instrument provided in Table 7.2.

THE PREVIOUS CHAPTERS ESTABLISHED a philosophical foundation for a Christian apologetic educational program. This chapter suggests a curriculum model for implementing apologetics in a Christian school curriculum at the secondary school level. We first discuss the nature of curriculum and instruction that takes place at the secondary school level. Then we suggest a model that integrates apologetics as a distinct subject of study into the curriculum. Finally, we suggest a conceptual model or framework for the subject of apologetics around which curriculum instructional materials can be developed.

THE NATURE OF CURRICULUM

Although we have used the term several times, it is important at this point to clearly identify what is meant by the term *curriculum*.[1] Lawrence

---

1. Some approaches would prefer the term "course of study" or even "syllabus" to preserve the term "curriculum" to apply instead to the entire experience of the student, even beyond what is described under a formal education.

Richards identifies curriculum as "the course of direction set by a teacher through which the student is to progress educationally. Curriculum is the sum of all of the experiences of the teaching-learning process. In its simplest terms, *curriculum* is the content that you plan to teach."[2] While the term can be used to designate learning experiences in or outside the class room, within education there is both an intrinsic and utility value to knowledge gained through curricular instruction. Educational knowledge can serve the student by helping him or her understand God's revelation (general and special) and use this to learn skills needed for gainful employment in the world. These two aspects of education have come to be termed in curriculum as Liberal and Vocational education.

Liberal vs. Vocational Education

Originally liberal education was so termed to emphasis the desire to develop within the student a free and critical mind. Most colleges have adapted the description of liberal education to refer to a broad selection of courses that may be required because they are believed to help developing the free and critical mind. However, some have suggested that the original concept of a free and critical mind should be used even at the secondary school level.[3] Unfortunately, much of what falls under the description of liberal education today is viewed as a platform on which all views are held to be equally valid and truth is relative. Hence, a definite Christian commitment to this kind of liberal education is not possible. However, as Willard M. Aldrich remarked in an article in 1962, "A liberal arts education with its music, art, literature, histories, and science, contributes to the enrichment of the soul. But the soul is liberated, and the soul integrated in rich development of personality only when such education is Christ-centered."[4] So it is not beyond the scope of Christian education to develop a truly liberal education, especially given God's general revelation.

The utility aspect of education is vocational (technical) or professional studies. Regardless of the level of instruction (i.e., secondary, undergraduate, graduate, etc) this course of study offers a selection of classes that prepare an individual for a specific career that they are ex-

2. Richards and Bredfeldt, *Creative Bible Teaching*, 198.

3. Adler, *Paideia Proposal*.

4. Aldrich, "Basic Concepts of Bible College Education," 248.

pected be able to enter upon graduation. This course of study may be combined with a liberal education, or it may stand alone depending on the kind of diploma, degree, certificate, etc. that is being pursued.

At the secondary level, sometimes the term general education is used to reference a "core" of courses that are considered standard or required by all students. James Johnson, in his text on American education, describes this as "the broad area of the school program that is concerned primarily with developing common learning."[5] If any particular subject is considered a part of the general education, then it is usually believed that every student should be exposed to the subject. This does not mean that every subject in the general education is equal in importance, but it does suggest that the subject is important enough to initially expose all students to regardless of the class duration. There may be courses taught that are not required for all students to take. These may be termed elective courses that survive mainly on the interest of students that creates a demand for them.

Curriculum Domains

Curriculum, understood in the broadest sense of the term, expands across three domains. Philosopher Mortimer Adler identifies these as the Acquisition of Organized Knowledge (AOK), Development of Intellectual Skills (DIS), and Understanding of Ideas and Values (UIV).[6] The AOK constitutes formalized instruction in the core curriculum such as language, literature, fine arts, mathematics, natural sciences, history, geography and social studies. The DIS primarily concerns the skills necessary to developing intellect. These would include the basic skills of learning needed in language and mathematics. These are foundational subjects that are integrated and necessary to all other subjects. Usually formal instruction is given in these areas throughout the secondary schooling. However, because of the foundational aspect of language and mathematics, skills and competency is constantly being developed through most of the courses covered in AOK. UIV concerns the development of attitudes and values that appreciate the end products (poetry, music, paintings, artists, etc.) and contributions (books, ideas, theories, etc.) made in the various subjects of learning. Auxiliary areas are some-

---

5. Johnson, et al., *Introduction to the Foundations of American Education*, 462.

6. Adler, *Paideia Proposal*, 22–23.

times added to the curriculum that includes such activities as physical training or health related subjects.

Within each of these domains of the curriculum there are various means and operations that take place to provide formal instruction. Some of these means include didactic instruction, lectures and responses, textbooks and other aids, coaching, exercises, supervised practice, questioning, active participation, etc. Operations include reading, writing, speaking, listening, calculating, problem-solving, measuring, estimating, judging, discussions, involvement, etc.

The level, intensity, and appropriateness of these means and operations must be judged by the teacher to achieve various goals or objectives in the curriculum (see Figure 7.1). Apologetics, as presented here, will only be considered part of the AOK. But there is certainly application and extension to be made in other areas.

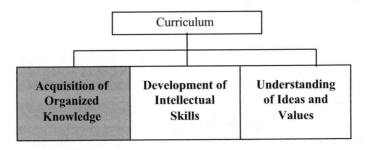

Figure 7.1 Curriculum Domains

Acquisition of Organized Knowledge

The infrastructure for the curriculum that includes the acquisition of organized knowledge begins at the foundation of mathematical and language subjects. These two areas of courses are foundational because they constitute areas that all other subjects and levels of learning are based upon. They also constitute the areas in which instruction and learning must be provided by another. In other words, one cannot learn language and mathematical skills unless someone teaches them. Upon this foundation, three broad areas of organized knowledge can be identified as humanities, sciences, and technologies. Within these three categories various individual subjects and courses can be devised to make up the general core curriculum.

CHRISTIAN EDUCATION CURRICULUM

The philosophy of Christian Apologetics Education suggested in chapter 3 concluded that apologetics should be a distinct subject of study. As such, its inclusion in the overall curriculum should be in the area of the acquisition of organized knowledge. Secondary schools, whether they are Christian or not, usually offer a core of classes that cover the humanities, sciences, and technologies. Beyond a different philosophical approach to each course, the Christian school usually requires, as a part of its core, a course or courses in religious instruction that centers in what may be termed biblical studies. In the model presented below, this is generally classified in the area of humanities.

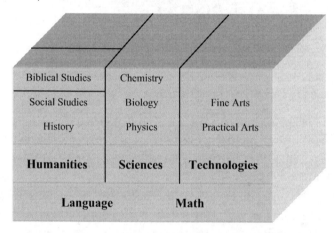

Figure 7.2 Taxonomy for the Acquisition of Organized Knowledge

Biblical studies may be further divided into various individual courses offered in theology and Bible. Theology may include subjects that take a topical or systematic approach. Such topics as Prolegomena, God, Christ, Sin, Salvation, the Church, and End Times are normal divisions made in theology. Other subjects may be in the area of practical ministry such as evangelism or discipleship. The area of Bible may include survey courses of the Old and New Testament. Other courses may exist in individual books of the Bible, authors, or even historical periods may play a role in the area of Bible. Regardless of courses offered in biblical studies or theology and Bible, the subject of apologetics clearly presents itself as a foundational subject to all biblical study subjects. Apologetics as a subject or body of knowledge (science) attempts to demonstrate the truth of the Christian religion. Hence, it is logically prior to the study of all other subjects classified as biblical studies.

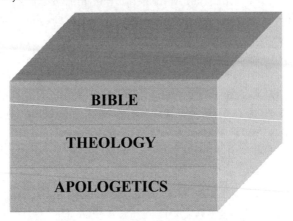

Figure 7.3 Taxonomy for Biblical Studies

THE NATURE OF APOLOGETICS AS A SUBJECT OF STUDY

The nature of apologetics as a subject of study tends to easily fit or fill a question and answer approach. Even the scriptures suggest the nature of this approach since the Christian is "to be ready . . . to give an answer" (1 Pet 3:15). Many texts on apologetics present the subject in this manner. It therefore, becomes quite easy for the teacher to assume this Socratic method of teaching as well. However, it is also important to recognize the subject as having an overall point, argument, or presentation to make that directs the student to the body of knowledge that makes the conclusion that Christianity alone is the true religion. As Etienne Gilson noted in lecture on education, there really is no fundamental difference between the exposition or lecture and the Socratic question and answer method because of "the fundamental facts of nature is that no man can understand anything for another one. . . . The only thing he can do is to help them to put it themselves into their own minds."[7] Regardless of the method, one should realize that the answer to apologetic questions does not lie in the student unless it is first learned or acquired by them. A teacher who is prepared with the answers to teach others that do not know the answers best accomplishes this.

7. Gilson, "The Eminence of Teaching," 24.

Although apologetics may take from any subject or discipline in order to defend the Christian faith, the two step approach of the classical method primarily draws from the arguments and evidence found in the subjects of philosophy and history. An understanding of the different methods and conclusion of these subjects will be important to developing a sound model of Christian Apologetics Education. Philosophy uses deductive reasoning that argues from specific premises to a general but necessary conclusion. For example, to argue for the existence of God, an argument might be stated:

1. The universe had a beginning.

2. Everything that has a beginning needs a cause.

3. Therefore, the universe needs a cause.

As long as the form of the argument is properly constructed (formal logic) and the premises correspond to reality (material logic), then the conclusion is necessary or undeniable.

History uses inductive reasoning that argues from general statements to a specific conclusion or to another general conclusion. A historical methodology and the world view of the historian are very important. For example, an atheistic-historian does not acknowledge the possibility of miracles and will never conclude that God raised Jesus from the dead (i.e., a miracle). The question of miracles (their possibility or actuality) is prior to the historical methodology and collection of evidence. In other words, it is a philosophical or world view problem and must be settled prior to the investigation of history. A historian with a theistic world view, on the other hand, can recognize the possibility that miracles might have happened since there is a God to act in the world. Using the proper methodology and techniques the theistic-historian has a world view that allows for the discovery of evidence for a possible miracle, while the atheist does not.

Philosophy and history use different reasoning and methods to arrive at different certitudes regarding their conclusions. Philosophy can yield necessary conclusions if the argument is valid (constructed properly) and true (premises correspond to reality). History on the other hand, yields probable or at best highly probable conclusions based on the available evidence and proper methodology.

Another aspect of apologetics that seems integral to teaching and doing apologetics is the reliance upon authorities or the making of appeals to authorities to demonstrate main points. While in some cases this can be over used, abused, or even result in an informal logical fallacy. Most who teach apologetics cannot be experts in every field or subject needed to make the whole case for Christian faith. Therefore, appeals to those more qualified to make certain points or reinforce conclusions are usually necessary. Such authorities may not always be favorable towards the Christian faith. Using the expert opinions of those, who are not Christian or even those who oppose an evangelical (or orthodox) theology, but favor the apologetic point, can be quite important and persuasive.

A Model for Apologetics

The classical apologetics methodology, for the purposes of an educational curriculum must be given a conceptual model for which instruction can be delivered and educational materials can be created. This approach to apologetics can be thought of as three necessary steps leading to the ultimate goal, which is demonstrating the truth of Christianity.

Philosophical Foundation. The first step deals with subjects in the area of Philosophy. Philosophy serves as a foundation for the entire task of apologetics. In the philosophical foundation, we ask and answer questions about reality, truth, knowledge, and first principles upon which arguments for God's existence can be constructed. Central to this step is the understanding of self-defeating propositions. For example, reality is knowable because it is impossible to affirm its opposite: "There is no such thing as reality" is a self-defeating statement. It affirms the reality of the statement in its denial. Likewise, truth must be absolute to be knowable. This is because all the conclusions in any area of knowledge must be based on or reducible to first principles. In other words, they are the beginning point of demonstration. If there was no such beginning point then there would be an infinite regress of knowledge and truth and impossible to demonstrate any truth. First principles, by their very nature are self-evident and undeniable. They are statements that are true in themselves. There really is no "defense" of them. Once they are understood, their truth can only be affirmed since to deny them is to use or rely upon their assertions.

Furthermore, there are at least two tests for truth. These are the tests of unaffirmability and undeniability. Unaffirmability refers to the inability to actually affirm something is true. For example if I say, "I cannot speak a word of English." The assertion clearly self destructs or is self-defeating. Undeniability refers to the ability to affirm something, which is actually universally necessarily true or unable to be shown false: hence undeniable. These are first principles such as the assertion: "something exists." These two tests for truth enable one either to show how something is self-destroyed or to affirm a universal ground on which to constrict an argument or to show how a truth is reducible to something that actually is undeniable.

Existence of God. The second stage builds upon this foundation by asking and answering questions about world views, the existence of God, of miracles, and the problem of evil. Here our apologetic must adjudicate between competing world views. Demonstrate that God exists and is the same God of Scripture. This should at least use the vertical and horizontal cosmological, teleological and moral arguments. Show that miracles are actual and discoverable as confirming acts of God. And finally, understand that evil, as problematic as it may be, is not a problem for the existence of the Christian God.

Truth of Christianity. The final or third stage asks and answers questions about the truth of Christianity. Here, questions concerning the reliability of the Bible and historicity of Jesus' life, teaching, and miracles are defended. This last step must also include Jesus' historical claim to be God and evidence of his bodily resurrection from the dead. This must form the central conclusion of any apologetic. At this secondary level this step should also incorporate a defense of Christian beliefs and ethics. While technically this may lie outside the bounds of apologetics, it is important for the student to grasp the supporting and clarifying role apologetics plays to Christian theology and ethics. The first two steps are concerned with questions of a philosophical nature in subjects such as metaphysics, epistemology and philosophy of religion. The final step concerns questions and subjects that are defended by historical and theological arguments. Figure 7.4 illustrates these three steps.[8]

---

8. Adapted from Howe *AP10 Problems in Apologetics.* Used by permission.

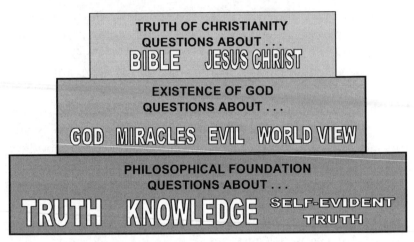

Figure 7.4 Tasks of Apologetics

Role of the Teacher and Student

Apologetics is a subject related to biblical and theological studies. It is, however, broader taking in truth wherever it may be found in general revelation. All that corresponds to reality is true and may be used to formulate a defense (apologetics) and explanation (theological) of the Christian faith. Apologetics as a subject is distinct and different from other subjects. Areas are covered where students, because of individual differences, upbringing, and denomination, will have particular questions that are sometimes of a deep spiritual and emotional concern. Students also may not always agree with either the teacher or other students on certain answers. Unlike some modern day approaches to education, apologetics does contain right or true answers to several major areas of study. While the formulation or expression of these answers may differ, there is only one right answer to important apologetic questions. For example, the answer to the question, "Do arguments prove God's existence?" Is, yes! However, how an argument is stated or even which argument(s) may be used to answer this question may vary.

Apologetics is a human enterprise and prone to have difficulties and controversies. While these can be explored in a healthy Christ-centered environment, it is important not to be too proud of one's ability to answers and shame another for not knowing or remembering. The teacher is the authority and either has the answer or the means to get the answer. Yet, this should not negate the teaching from engaging the class in exercise that places the student in a simulated authoritative position where they can practice apologetics. The teacher must also set the boundary that the study of apologetics covers is appropriate to the age level and experience of the student. However, students should be given some input into the questions that are raised, issues covered, and even activities that are done. For example, the teacher may include in the course of study arguments for the existence of God. The student has no choice concerning the topic, but should have input concerning questions and objections that might be raised about the topic that need to be answered.

Another area of caution concerns intellectual ability of the student and the need for wisdom when applying apologetics. Since students will vary in their analytical abilities, it is the responsibility of the teacher to deliver only what the student is able to process at their intellectual level and applies to their level of maturity. Hence, the teacher must make judgments about the student's ability to wisely use apologetics. For example, a student with a high analytical ability and a "go beat them (unbelievers) up attitude" will need more work in the area of "with gentleness and reverence" (1 Pet 3:15) as opposed to "be ready to defend." Likewise, a timid student with less analytical ability may need to have the reverse to be emphasized.

Finally, ministry opportunities such as evangelism or other practical application for the student and teacher should play an important role in a class on apologetics. This will help to make the course meaningful to the students and involve them at a personal level.

Role of the Textbook

The nature of the subject of apologetics as well as the offering of the subject as a distinct course makes it strongly advisable, if not necessary, to use a textbook. A textbook is an important part of the instructional process. It gives students the necessary background to understand the subject of apologetics. Just as it is not the intent of a course on physical science at the secondary school level to make the student into a professional scientist, it is not the intent of a course on apologetics to make the student into a professional apologist. However, it is important to expose the student to the basic thoughts, ideas, and themes that concern the subject of apologetics. This will help ensure that students are exposed to this area of study for which the Scriptures give an imperative to be ready with an answer (1 Pet 3:15). The textbook is indispensable towards this end.

The textbook also, as in other courses, should be used to deliver the basic content of the subject. It should serve as a source for regular reading assignments, quizzes, and reviews. It should be brought to class each day and be used as a resource for class activities, assignments, and projects.

Selection of the Textbook

The text book should play a central role in any course that has a specific level or amount of organized knowledge to be mastered. Short of a teacher writing his or her own text, or creating an anthology, a textbook must be selected. The following instrument can be used to evaluate potential books that cover the subject of apologetics in order to assess which books might be the most appropriate for use at the secondary school level. Books on apologetics that present themselves as college level or above should not be considered for the secondary student. It should be understood that many books published in the area of apologetics at a popular level are not written as a secondary school textbook. Some are also written on specialized topics but are not comprehensive. This does bring up the possibility of combing texts in various areas of apologetics to serve as textbooks. While this may be possible, it would be undesirable for the sake of convenience at this age level. It is imperative to demonstrate continuity of subject matter, and the presentation format of information. Many are written as books of interest to the young or lay reader and some are designed for small groups. Hence, this selection process is not intended to pass negative judgment on any author or publisher for not doing a better job. Publishers must have a market to sell books, and the fact that there may be few books fitting the needs of a secondary school teacher in apologetics, only shows that apologetics, as we have described it in this book, may be very rare in the Christian secondary level. The fact that there are several textbooks on apologetics at the college and seminary level would seem to reinforce this point. Furthermore, it is important to realize that if a book does not meet the criterion used here, it does not mean the book has no value or that it has no place in an apologetics course. Many of these books may be excellent resources in a secondary school apologetics class for the teacher and student.

Richard T. and Jo Anne L. Vacca, in their book *Content Area Reading*, identify that the "primary purpose of a textbook is to provide users with information."[9] They also identify two areas of assessment:

9. Vacca and Vacca, *Content Area Reading*, 185.

Internal and external organization. Internal refers to the subject matter, its interrelationship, and subordination of ideas in the text. External refers to features or organizational aids that facilitate reading. These would include all front and end matter of the book (e.g., preface, table of contents, appendices, bibliography and index, etc.). It also includes each chapter of a textbook that should have an introduction/summary statement, headings, graphs, charts, illustrations, and guide questions that relate to the content.

Another area of evaluation is readability. While readability tests cannot test how easily a reader can understand information in a text, it can give a quick assessment about the density and level of writing. There are several readability tests.[10] For this assessment, the Flesch readability test and the Flesch-Kinkaid grade level estimate is suggested for use. This is a readability estimate built into some word processing programs. The Flesch readability test measures readability on a scale from 0 to 100 (see Table 7.1). Zero is the hardest level and 100 is the easiest level. Sixty five (65) is understood to be average or normal readability.

100	Very easy to read	Average sentence length is 12 words or less. No words of more than two syllables.
65	Average	Average sentence length is 15 to 20 words. Average word has two syllables.
0	Extremely difficult to read	Average sentence length is 37 words. Average word has more than two syllables.

Table 7.1 Flesch Readability Test

The Flesch-Kincaid grade level computes readability based on the average number of syllables per word and the average number of words per sentence. The score produced corresponds directly to the grade level. For example, a score of 8.0 would be an eighth grade reading level. Three passages, from the beginning, middle and end of the text should be randomly selected. Such passages should avoid any quotations of authors and should consist of approximately one hundred words each. The Flesh

10. See ibid., 49–58. If word processing capabilities are not available, the Fry test is appropriate for use, see ibid. There are some tests that should only be used for primary school books. The Flesch-Kinkaid is appropriate for secondary school text assessment and is the only test sanctioned by the USA Government. See "Readability" [available on-line] http://www.timetabler.com/reading.html accessed 21 January 2005.

readability and Flesch-Kincaid grade level estimate can be applied by using some word processing programs.

There are other areas of consideration such as the interest level and any motivating features of the content of the text. Additionally one can consider the legibility of print, type (e.g., use of boldface, italic or capitals for emphasis), layout (e.g., artistic value), and sentence structure.

APOLOGETICS TEXTBOOK ASSESSMENT CRITERIA

Internal

I. The internal assessment of the text:

    A. Fit the classical methodology of apologetics by:

        1. Addresses existence of God and the theistic world view;

        2. Addresses other world views opposed to Theism;

        3. Addresses the historical truth of Christianity.

    B. Provides content that covers the subject in a systematic manner by:

        1. Integrates apologetic information into an overall argument for Christianity;

        2. Addresses significant objections to the Christian faith and/ or answers problems and questions.

II. Reading Level Assessment: At the appropriate reading level or slightly lower:

    A. Flesch readability test around 65 or better;

    B. Flesch-Kinkaid Grade Level (between 8–12 grades).

External

III. The external organization of the text:

    A. Provides an introduction/summary statement for each chapter;

    B. Provides instructional objectives for each chapter that cover the content of the chapter;

C. Provides review or guide questions at the end or beginning of each chapter

D. Questions and objectives help reinforce and analyze the subject material of the text;

E. Makes use of multi-level headings for each chapter;

F. Makes use of various pictures, tables, charts, illustrations that reinforce the subject content discussed in each chapter of the text;

G. Suggests further books and/or resources for further study in each chapter;

H. Provides end matter that contains an index, table of contents, and glossary.

Ideally, a textbook on apologetics should meet the following apologetic and educational characteristics. First, it should fit the classical methodology of apologetics established in Chapter 2. At a very minimum, it should present a methodology that does not ignore or counter the classical approach to apologetic education. This would include addressing arguments for the existence of God, why the theistic world view is true and other world views are false. Second, it should present Christianity as historically true. Third, it should provide content that covers the subject in a systematic manner. This is opposed to only dealing with some questions or not showing how apologetics makes a comprehensive, i.e., full, argument for the truth of the Christian faith. Fourth, it should be at the appropriate reading level of the secondary school student (grades 9–12) or slightly lower. A slightly lower reading level, especially for new subjects, is actually more desirable to help communicate some difficult material. Fifth, it should provide an introduction or summary statement for each chapter. Sixth, it should provide instructional objectives at the beginning of each chapter stated in terms of what outcome is expected for the student. Seventh, it should provide guide questions at the end or beginning of each chapter. Eighth, it should make use of multi-level headings in each chapter. Ninth, it should employ various pictures, tables, charts, illustrations and other visual aids to reinforce the subject content. Tenth, is should suggest further books or resources for students and teachers. Finally, it should provide front and end matter that contains an index, table of contents, and glossary. These eleven criteria are offered in degrees of importance. This means the first criteria are more important than successive criterion. Yet, the entire list is desirable in an apologetics text.

Over the years I have been involved with apologetics, I have searched for a text that comes closest to meeting this criterion. The best text, in my estimation, is *When Skeptics Ask* by Norman L. Geisler and Ronald M. Brooks.[11] I have therefore decided, for the purposes of demonstration, to wrap the curriculum materials around this particular text. The Christian educator is encouraged to review other potential apologetic texts for the sake of comparison. However, for the purposes of illustration we will examine this text by applying the above criterion. On a scale from 1–7 (7 being the best, 1 being the worst, and 0 indicating the item is not present) I have evaluated the text according to each stated criterion. The textbook evaluation results are recorded below (Table 7.3). The educator is encouraged to do his or her own evaluation of this and other textbooks to give a total comparison.

---

11. Geisler and Brooks, *When Skeptics Ask*, 29.

		TEXT BOOK TITLES							
		When Skeptics Ask							
INTERNAL ASSESSMENT CRITERION	WORLD VIEWS	7							
	NON–THEISTIC WORLD VIEWS	6							
	EXISTENCE & NATURE OF GOD	6							
	HISTORICAL TRUTH OF CHRISTIANITY	7							
	OVERALL ARGUMENT FOR CHRISTIANITY	7							
	ANSWERS OBJECTIONS TO CHRISTIANITY	7							
	READABILITY	6							
	GRADE LEVEL	6							
EXTERNAL ORGANIZATIONAL ASSESSMENT	INTRODUCTIONS	0							
	CHAPTER OBJECTIVES	0							
	CHAPTER SUMMARIES	4							
	REVIEW QUESTIONS	0							
	MULTI–LEVEL HEADINGS	6							
	GRAPHICS	6							
	SUGGESTED READINGS	6							
	INDEX	7							
	TABLE OF CONTENTS	7							
	GLOSSARY	7							
	TOTAL SCORE:	95							

Table 7.2 Apologetics Textbook Analysis Chart

This text was selected for a number of reasons. First, it fits the classical as well as systematic criterion mentioned above. This text does many important things that other texts at this level fail to do well. For example, it presents all the possible world views and contrasts them with Christianity.[12] It is laid out in a question and answer format.[13] It connects philosophical arguments for the existence and nature of God with the Theistic God of the Bible; and it provides an overall argument for the Christian faith that shows how each chapter contributes to the argument.[14]

Second, it is written at the target age level of this curriculum (grade 9–12). It has a normal reading level and shows Flesch-Kinkaid a Grade level of 8.4 and a Flesch Readability Score of 60. Third, it uses multi-level headings in each chapter. Fourth, it contains summaries at the end of each chapter. Fifth, it contains many illustrations, charts, pictures, graphs, and sidebar issues. Sixth, it suggests further readings for each chapter. Seventh, it contains a topical and scriptural index, table of contents, and glossary. All of these will greatly enhance the students learning and the teacher's ability to relate subject matter.

The text, however, does have some shortcomings that are important to note. First, it may not have been written specifically to be a "textbook" regardless of the level. That being the case, it may explain why it does not contain chapter objectives and guide questions. It lacks some sections that are important in studying apologetics. For example, there is no chapter on the history of apologetics or apologetic methods. Another problem is the order of some chapters may not be conducive to a systematic course in apologetics. For example, chapter twelve on truth is towards the end of the book when it might need to be covered earlier in the course. However, a curriculum can be designed to compensate for these weaknesses. Given that most texts, that cover the subject at this level, are not classical or systematic, this is a good and adequate text for instruction.

This chapter established specifically how the subject of apologetics can fit into the secondary school curriculum. Apologetics is presented as a foundational subject to biblical studies. The apologetic model suggested covers and integrates topics in a Philosophical foundation, God,

12. Ibid., 35–37.
13. Ibid., Contents.
14. Ibid., 26–29; 291–92.

and Christianity. In the next chapter, we cover specific materials a curriculum needs to facilitate the educational process of apologetics.

QUESTIONS TO ANSWER

1. Why is apologetics so foundational to other biblical and theological subjects?

2. Discuss any advantages or disadvantages concerning the curriculum model for apologetics.

3. Evaluate an apologetics textbook according to the instrument provided in Table 7.3.

SELECT READINGS

Norman L. Geisler and Ronald M. Brooks, *When Skeptics Ask.*

8

Curriculum Materials Needed
for Christian Apologetics Education

OBJECTIVES

Evaluate general and specific objectives for teaching apologetics at the secondary school level.

Explain how apologetics, as a subject of study, can be integrated into other disciples.

IN THIS CHAPTER, WE build upon the model and text suggested in the previous chapter for a Christian apologetics educational program. A curriculum needs to contain various materials and components that the teacher of apologetics can draw upon to develop and implement a successful class. While an entire manual is beyond the scope of this present book, a sample unit is provided to complete the picture of what is needed. The apologetics teacher is encouraged to use this as a guide for developing their own curriculum materials for use in the course.

INTRODUCTION TO THE CURRICULUM

The instructional curriculum should be developed with specific roles for the student, teacher, textbook, and manual in mind. The curriculum manual for apologetics should work as an aid to teachers. Hence, it is a suggestion on how the course might be taught. The final decision on what to teach and how to teach rests with the teacher. The teacher is responsible for selecting, delivering, and evaluating student learning.

To assist the teacher, a manual should serve the following purposes:

1. Offer a rationale for teaching apologetics in a systematic classical approach.

2. Presents general and specific unit objectives to be used to form a conceptual structure for various topics.

3. Presents information, activities, instructional aids, and evaluation materials.

4. Help integrate other subjects into the study of apologetics.

5. Lists references for teacher information and further education.

The manual along with the text should be read and studied by the teacher well in advance of implementing the course or developing lessons. The manual should contain suggestions and aids to designing an exciting class on apologetics. It should be designed for flexibility and to facilitate an apologetics program that will interest a wide variety of students.

A curriculum manual for apologetics should be designed to teach apologetics in a systematic approach. This means that the materials are designed to cover the complete subject (Jude 3) and to be an apologetics for the Christian faith (1 Peter 3:15). It is based on the belief that Christian apologetics should be taught as a distinct subject, similar to other subjects (e.g., math, science, or Bible). Hence, apologetics should be considered a part of general Christian education.

The instructional curriculum should be divided into units. Each unit should provide six sections and instructional materials for each of the thirteen units. The first section contains a general *Unit Objective* and *Specific Objectives*. The second section contains *Suggested Activities* and *Resources* for published written, audio, and visual aids. The third section contains *Information Sheets* to be used by the students to help take notes, listen to lessons and presentations, and study for tests. The fourth section contains *Transparency* masters or digital files for instructional use in a software presentation program. The fifth section contains *Assignment Sheets* for group or individual activities. The sixth section contains the unit *Test* or evaluation materials and answer sheets. The following units of instruction can be combined with the curriculum model and text as follows:

I.   Unit 1-A Introduction to Apologetics (text chapter 1)

PHILOSOPHICAL FOUNDATION: TRUTH

II.   Unit 1-B TRUTH (text chapter 12)

EXISTENCE OF GOD: THEISM

III.   Unit 2-A GOD (text chapter 2)

IV.   Unit 2-B WORLD VIEWS (text chapter 3)

V.   Unit 2-C PROBLEM OF EVIL (text chapter 4)

VI.   Unit 2-D MIRACLES (text chapter 5)

TRUTH OF CHRISTIANITY: HISTORICAL APOLOGETICS

VII.   Unit 3-A THE BIBLE (text chapter 7)

VIII.   Unit 3-B JESUS CHRIST (text chapter 6)

TRUTH OF CHRISTIANITY: DEFENDING CHRISTIAN BELIEF

IX.   Unit 3-C BIBLE DIFFICULTIES (text chapter 8)

X.   Unit 3-D ARCHEOLOGY (text chapter 9)

XI.   Unit 3-E SCIENCE AND EVOLUTION (text chapter 10)

XII.   Unit 3-F DEATH AND THE AFTERLIFE (text chapter 11)

XIII.   Unit 3-G ETHICS (text chapter 13)

Appendix: ARGUMENT FOR CHRISTIANITY (text Appendix)

Each unit can be classified according to a typical 18 week semester as follows:

Unit	Title	Text Chapter	Week(s)	
1–A	INTRODUCTION	1	1	
1–B	TRUTH	12	1	
2–A	GOD	2	1	
2–B	WORLD VIEWS	3	2	
2–C	PROBLEM OF EVIL	4	2	
2–D	MIRACLES	5	1	
3–A	THE BIBLE	7	2	
3–B	JESUS CHRIST	6	1	18 Week Semester
3–C	BIBLE DIFFICULTIES	8	1	
3–D	ARCHEOLOGY	9	1	
3–E	SCIENCE AND EVOLUTION	10	1	
3–F	DEATH AND THE AFTERLIFE	11	1	
3–G	ETHICS	13	1	
Appendix	ARGUMENT FOR CHRISTIANITY	Appendix	1	
Unassigned			1	

Table 8.1 Apologetics Semester Schedule

GOALS OF CHRISTIAN APOLOGETICS EDUCATION

The following are general goals of a Christian Apologetics Educational Program. The term "goals" are sometimes used interchangeable with "objectives." For our purposes here, *goals* should be understood as general to what the student should develop as a result of the entire CAE program, while *objectives* are more specific to outcomes expected in a particular unit of instruction. They are provided for the purposes of helping the apologetics educator develop, organize, classify, and justify instructional content.

1. Describes the origin and historical development of apologetics in Church history.

2. Relates the importance of apologetics to the Christian faith.

3. Successfully communicates important apologetic terms, facts, ideas, and arguments.

4. Successfully uses important apologetic terms, facts, ideas, and arguments to defend and explain the Christian faith.

5. Appreciates the importance of Christian ethics in the defense of the Christian faith.

6. Recognizes and critiques various non-Christian world views, religions, cults and their theology and arguments.

7. Selects appropriate apologetic arguments to answer the objections of opponents to the Christian faith.

8. Combines and uses various apologetic arguments in dialogue with opponents (or those representing the opponents) to the Christian faith.

INSTRUCTIONAL ANALYSIS
OF CHRISTIAN APOLOGETICS EDUCATION

These objectives should be presented at the beginning of each unit. This kind of objective is a summary statement of what is to be achieved in terms of the student. It is given for each unit followed by a breakdown of each specific objective classified according to the traditional domains of cognitive, psychomotor, and affective. This is offered to help in the planning of instructional content by the apologetic teacher. The Christian educator should be responsible for integrating appropriate spiritual outcomes. They should also adapt these objectives to a more specific outcome description that would fit their individual student needs and instructional setting.

Specific Outcome Objectives:
I. Introduction to Apologetics Unit 1-A

After completion of this unit, the student should be able to distinguish between the tasks of apologetics, discuss how they relate to apologetics, and utilize apologetics to solve a problem or objection to Christianity.

RELATED TO INFORMATION: What the Student should know (Cognitive)	PRACTICAL APPLICATION: What the Student should be able to do (Psychomotor)	RELATED TO EMOTIONS: What the Student should be able to feel (Affective)
1. Defines Christian Apologetic terms.		
2. States self-evident truths.		
3. Identifies self-referential statements.		
4. Describes the difference between evangelism and pre-evangelism.		
5. States and explains important Bible verses on apologetics.		
6. Identifies major figures in the history of apologetics.		
	7. Identifies uses for Apologetics in the Community or Church.	
	8. Discusses how the stages of Apologetic reasoning relate to each other.	
		9. Responds to an Apologetic problem in a group setting.

Specific Outcome Objectives:
II. Truth Unit 1-B

After completion of this unit the student should be able to define truth, theories about truth, defend the correct view of truth, and appreciate the relationship between truth and apologetics.

RELATED TO INFORMATION: What the Student should know (Cognitive)	PRACTICAL APPLICATION: What the Student should be able to do (Psychomotor)	RELATED TO EMOTIONS: What the Student should be able to feel (Affective)
1. Defines terms related to truth. 2. Defines the two major theories of truth.		
	3. Defends the correspondence view of truth. 4. Discusses the challenges of Postmodernism.	
		5. Appreciates the relationship between self-evident truths and Apologetic ends.

Specific Outcome Objectives: III. God Unit 2-A

After completion of this unit, the student should be able to properly use rational arguments for God's existence, explain how this is the same God described in the Bible, and answer objections or questions about God's existence.

RELATED TO INFORMATION: What the Student should know (Cognitive)	PRACTICAL APPLICATION: What the Student should be able to do (Psychomotor)	RELATED TO EMOTIONS: What the Student should be able to feel (Affective)
1. Identifies four arguments for the existence of God. 2. Uses and explains an argument for the existence of God.		
	3. Explains the connection between an argument for God's existence and God as described in the Bible	
	4. Criticizes and answers objections to the existence of God.	
		5. Assess the need and placement of proving the existence of God.

Specific Outcome Objectives: IV. World Views Unit 2-B

After completion of this unit, the student should be able to distinguish between the seven world views, discuss their beliefs about God, the world, evil, and ethics and be able to critique each view opposed to Theism.

RELATED TO INFORMATION: What the Student should know (Cognitive)	PRACTICAL APPLICATION: What the Student should be able to do (Psychomotor)	RELATED TO EMOTIONS: What the Student should be able to feel (Affective)
1. Describes seven major world views. 2. Identifies seven major world views and their corresponding beliefs about God, the world and morality.		
	3. Criticizes and examines seven major world views.	
		4. Provides answers to representatives of a world view opposed to Theism.

Specific Outcome Objectives: V. Problem of Evil Unit 2-C

After completion of this unit, the student should be able to describe the problem of evil, identify answers to the problem, demonstrate how the problem is compatible with the nature of God and proves the existence God, and develop an awareness of the solution apologetics gives to the human problem of evil.

RELATED TO INFORMATION: What the Student should know (Cognitive)	PRACTICAL APPLICATION: What the Student should be able to do (Psychomotor)	RELATED TO EMOTIONS: What the Student should be able to feel (Affective)
1. Describes the problem of evil in terms of its nature, origin, persistence, purpose, and amount.		
2. Identifies and discusses an answer to the four problem areas or objections concerning evil.		
	3. Demonstrates how the problem of evil can be used as a proof for the existence of God.	
		4. Use the idea of possible worlds to answer objections concerning the compatibility of God and Evil
		5. Develops an awareness of the human problem of evil and the solution apologetics offers.

Specific Outcome Objectives: VI. Miracles Unit 2-D

After completion of this unit the student should be able to define terms associated with miracles, describe various objections to miracles and give answers, demonstrate the apologetic value of miracles and relate the contributions of significant thinkers to the issue of miracles.

RELATED TO INFORMATION: What the Student should know (Cognitive)	PRACTICAL APPLICATION: What the Student should be able to do (Psychomotor)	RELATED TO EMOTIONS: What the Student should be able to feel (Affective)
1. Defines terms related to miracles. 2. Describes objections to miracles in the realm of their possibility, credibility, scientificity, historicity, mythology, identifiability and value. 3. Identifies and describes answers to the seven areas of objections to miracles.	4. Demonstrates the apologetics application and value of miracles.	5. Relates the contributions of a significant thinker concerning miracles.

Specific Outcome Objectives: VII. The Bible Unit 3-A

After completion of this unit the student should be able to define terms related to Bibliology, identify important historical development of the history and transmission of the Bible, describe the reliability and inspiration of the Bible, respond to various objections to the reliability of the Bible, and recognize the important role biblical history has in apologetics.

RELATED TO INFORMATION: What the Student should know (Cognitive)	PRACTICAL APPLICATION: What the Student should be able to do (Psychomotor)	RELATED TO EMOTIONS: What the Student should be able to feel (Affective)
1. Defines terms related to the cannnonicity, inspiration and inerrancy of the Bible.		
2. Identifies the historical developments concerning the cannon of the Bible.		
3. Identifies the existence and value of various apocryphal and Gnostic Gospels.		
4. Identifies the transmission methods of the Bible.		
	5. Describes the overall argument that the Bible is the word of God.	
	6. Describes and demonstrates the reliability of the New Testament.	
	7. Describes and demonstrates the reliability of the Old Testament.	
	8. Describes and identifies the value of Jesus' testimony to the inspiration of the Bible.	
		9. Responds to objections leveled against the authenticity of the Bible.
		10. Recognizes the level of biblical historicity needed to achieve Apologetic ends.

Specific Outcome Objectives: VIII. Jesus Christ Unit 3-B

After completion of this unit the student should be able to state the evidence related to the claim of Jesus to be God, identify the correct doctrine and incorrect doctrines regarding the nature of Jesus, explore the evidence for the physical resurrection of Jesus and answer objections, describe the proper role of history, problems and answers related to Jesus' Deity and resurrection.

RELATED TO INFORMATION: What the Student should know (Cognitive)	PRACTICAL APPLICATION: What the Student should be able to do (Psychomotor)	RELATED TO EMOTIONS: What the Student should be able to feel (Affective)
1. States the evidence for the claim of Jesus to be God in the New Testament.		
2. Identifies the Orthodox doctrine of the nature of Jesus Christ.		
3. Identifies false views of Jesus.		
4. Explores evidence related to the historical and physical resurrection of Jesus.		
5. Answers objections to the resurrection of Jesus.		
	6. Describes the proper role of presuppositions and historiography in the study of Jesus.	
	7. Describes problems and answers to objections regarding Jesus' Deity.	
		8. Provides answers to opposing views of the physical resurrection of Jesus.

Specific Outcome Objectives: IX. Bible Difficulties Unit 3-C

After completion of this unit the student should be able to identify guidelines for Bible difficulties, explains a contradiction and a difficulty, identifies various Bible difficulties, uses resources to solve a difficulty, and explores possible solutions.

RELATED TO INFORMATION: What the Student should know (Cognitive)	PRACTICAL APPLICATION: What the Student should be able to do (Psychomotor)	RELATED TO EMOTIONS: What the Student should be able to feel (Affective)
1. Identifies guidelines for handling Bible difficulties. 2. Explains the difference between a contradiction and a difficulty as it relates to the Bible. 3. Identifies various Bible difficulties.		
	4. Use various resources to develop solutions to Bible difficulties.	
		5. Explores various Bible difficulties and their possible solutions.

Specific Outcome Objectives: X. Archeology Unit 3-D

After completion of this unit the student should be able to define archeological terms, describe the value and limitations of archeology, use archeology to validate biblical claims, and explore archeological discoveries and their relationship to the Bible.

RELATED TO INFORMATION: What the Student should know (Cognitive)	PRACTICAL APPLICATION: What the Student should be able to do (Psychomotor)	RELATED TO EMOTIONS: What the Student should be able to feel (Affective)
1. Defines archeology and related terms. 2. Describes the values and limits of archeology as a tool in biblical study.		
	3. Uses archeology to validate biblical claims.	
		4. Explores various archeological discoveries and their relationship to the Bible.

Specific Outcome Objectives: XI. Science and Evolution Unit 3-E

After completion of this unit the student should be able to define terms involved in science, creation and evolution, explore the evidence for the origin of life, the universe, first life, and humans, discuss the evidence as related to creation and evolution, views and answers evolutionary assumptions and arguments.

RELATED TO INFORMATION: What the Student should know (Cognitive)	PRACTICAL APPLICATION: What the Student should be able to do (Psychomotor)	RELATED TO EMOTIONS: What the Student should be able to feel (Affective)
1. Defines creation and evolution. 2. Defines terms associated with Science and evolution. 3. Explores the scientific evidence for the origin of the universe, first life, and humans.		
	4. Discusses the strengths and weakness of scientific evidence as it relates to creation and evolution.	
		5. Views evolutionary media to criticize its evolutionary assumptions. 6. Answers an argument opposed to creation.

Specific Outcome Objectives: XII. Death and the Afterlife Unit 3-F

After completion of this unit the student should be able to write about the biblical evidence for a resurrection, describe the differences with re-incarnation and identify biblical descriptions of the afterlife, answer and criticize false views of the afterlife, and appreciate the hope of eternal life and the role of apologetics.

RELATED TO INFORMATION: What the Student Should Know (Cognitive)	PRACTICAL APPLICATION: What the Student should be able to do (Psychomotor)	RELATED TO EMOTIONS: What the Student should be able to feel (Affective)
1. Writes the biblical evidence for resurrection. 2. Describes the difference between resurrection and reincarnation. 3. Identifies the biblical descriptions of life after death.		
	4. Answers objections to reincarnation. 5. Criticizes and examines false views of the after life.	
		6. Appreciates the hope and solution eternal life provides the Christian. 7. Realizes the role death and the after-life can have in reaching apologetic ends.

Specific Outcome Objectives: XIII. Ethics Unit 3-G

After completion of this unit, the student should be able to define ethical terms and ethical theories, discuss conflicting and non-conflicting absolutism, relate Christian ethics to various issues, and appreciate the consequences of an unethical life.

RELATED TO INFORMATION: What the Student Should Know (Cognitive)	PRACTICAL APPLICATION: What the Student should be able to do (Psychomotor)	RELATED TO EMOTIONS: What the Student should be able to feel (Affective)
1. Defines terms related to ethics. 2. Defines absolute and non-absolute theories of ethics.		
	3. Discuses conflicting and non-conflicting views in relationship to Christianity. 4. Explores various problems and solutions to absolutism.	
		5. Relates Christian ethics to various ethical issues. 6. Appreciates the devastating ends that an unethical life can produce.

INTERDISCIPLINARY NATURE OF APOLOGETICS

Each unit has subject material that overlaps concepts taught in other subjects. The teacher should be aware of this material so it can be incorporated into lesson planning. The apologetic teacher should review with other teachers concerning units being taught that are common to other subjects so they can incorporate aspects of apologetics and vise versa that will reinforce other subjects and skills. We will review each subject to illustrate common material between subject matter.

Reading. Every unit because it has a corresponding chapter will involve reading. Each chapter will introduce new vocabulary words and corresponding definitions and concepts to the student of apologetics. Assignments should be given that cause the student to see these new words used in a written text. This along with review and testing of these vocabulary words will be important to ensure that learning, not just rote memorization, is taking place. Additional works such as published articles in magazines, newspapers, debates, etc. that touch on relevant issues should also be incorporated to help build the vocabulary of the student. There is a genre of apologetic literature. C. S. Lewis, perhaps the most well known popular literary author of apologetic works, could be read by apologetic students.[1]

Writing. Every unit of instruction can cause the student to engage in short and long, creative, informational, as well as persuasive writing assignments. This may include short answer questions, reports, debates, and research papers that will specifically cover an aspect of the field of apologetics. Such assignments may improve overall writing and grammatical skills. Developing a class newsletter on apologetics can give student the opportunity to fill various rolls associated with written media (such as journalist, reporter, editor, etc.).

Mathematics. Units 3A The Bible and 3E Creation and Evolution are the major units in which mathematics can be integrated. Numbers play a significant role in the biblical text. As professor John J. Davis suggests, "The subject of Biblical Numerology touches, in some way or another, every area in Biblical studies. The subject is vitally connected with the over-all field of theology and more specifically with the prophetic

---

1. See Lewis, *Mere Christianity, Miracles, The Problem of Pain, The Weight of Glory, The Great Divorce,* and *The Abolition of Man.* These as well as his fictional works may be appropriately read in conjunction with other subjects such as English or Literature classes.

doctrines of the Bible . . . for numbers, . . . are important not only in conveying mathematical data, but in formulating literary stylisms."[2] There are many things specific to apologetics that involve numbers and calculations. For example, the number of messianic prophecies that are given in the Old Testament and are fulfilled in the New can be used to calculate the probability that they could happen with any one person by chance.[3] The evidence for creation provides another opportunity to integrate mathematics. For example, it may be helpful to investigate the calculations related to the anthropic principle, which gives evidence of design in the universe and the unlikely hood of the smallest conceivable form of life arising by chance.[4] Some have taken numbers and mathematics to an unhealthy extreme by supposedly finding mysterious messages and prophesies hidden in the biblical texts. A class on apologetics can provide a defense against such abuses and model the proper role of numerology.

Communication. Every unit can emphasize the role in communication, especially oral, when doing apologetics. The communication skills learned and practiced here may include interpersonal and group. While apologetics may seem best suited to persuasive speeches, other forms such as informative and implicational can be used as well. The parts of a speech, audience considerations, and length should be considered. Class debates, group discussions, and question and answer session activities can be incorporated into any unit. Role playing, or doing it for real if the opportunity exists, as a media person (such as reporter, radio, TV personality, producer, etc.) who communicates apologetics issues can add motivation and excitement to the message and importance of apologetics.

Philosophy. Because the goal of philosophy is the pursuit of wisdom and the goal of apologetics is the rational demonstration of the truth of Christianity, there will be plenty of overlap. Almost every unit will touch some common aspect of the two disciplines. The basic subjects of philosophy include logic, metaphysics, epistemology, and ethics. Logic will be used whenever an argument, whether deductive or inductive, is being made. Examples of valid and true arguments can be contrasted with invalid and false arguments. Formal and informal fallacies can be explained. Whenever teaching concerns the existence and nature of God, metaphysics is being used. When teaching self-evident truths, and how

2. Davis, *Biblical Numerology*, 17.

3. See Geisler, "Prophecy, as Proof of the Bible," 609–617; and Stoner and Newman, *Science Speaks.*

4. See Ross, *The Fingerprint of God.*

humans know things, epistemology is involved. Various ethical systems may be contrasted with graded absolutism. Various ethical solutions to contemporary issues should be contrasted with the Christian solution. Many good Christian resources exist for the teacher to develop content and activities related to these philosophical and apologetic subjects.[5]

Science. Many aspects of apologetics will overlap scientific subjects. However, unit's 2-D Miracles, 3-D Archeology, and 3-E Science and Evolution naturally contain material relevant to scientific subjects. Our modern scientific mindset has raised objections to the possibility and actuality of miracles. Such objections therefore must be answered by the apologetics teacher through a proper understanding of the nature of the subjects involved and the naturalistic objections offered by science to the supernatural.[6] Archeology is a field of study that has not only shed light on an understanding of the biblical text, but has verified numerous biblical claims. The apologetic teacher needs to be aware of such discoveries for the purposes of establishing the reliability of the Old and New Testament. This is a crucial step in the overall argument for Christianity.[7] There is no more important area of intersection than that provided in the conflict between creation and evolution. The apologetic teacher should work closely with the science teacher to integrate the areas of origin regarding the universe (Earth Science), first life, and human life (Biology). Many biological details can overlap with an apologetic that incorporates evidence of intelligent design as well as a biblical defense of creationism.[8] As one popular scientific apologist stated, "Genesis 1–11 speaks of the history of the universe, Earth, life on Earth, and of humanity's origin and early development. With the help of many remarkable advances in astronomy, physics, geophysics, chemistry, paleontology, biochemistry, and anthropology, the words of the first eleven chapters can be subjected, point by point, to rigorous investigation"[9] As was stated earlier, two popular models of biblical creationism at present seem to dominate evangelical theology. They are progressive creationism, or day-age view, and the 24-hour or young earth view. While a particular teacher or school may favor one view over the other, the apol-

5. See Geisler and Feinberg, *Introduction to Philosophy*, and Geisler, *Christian Ethics.*

6. See Geisler, *Miracles and the Modern Mind*, 43–53.

7. Wilson, *Rocks, Relics and Biblical Reliability.*

8. Moreland, *The Creation Hypothesis.*

9. Ross, *The Genesis Question*, 10.

ogetic teacher, if possible, should present a summary of the scientific and biblical evidence for and against each view.[10] Admittedly, it is here that the student will see limitations and unresolved conflicts between the scientist and theologian. But ignoring this conflict cannot help the education or apologetics process.

History. While there is much history that overlaps the Bible, the apologist is mostly concerned with the Bible's historical reliability. The apologetics teacher can work with the history teacher to help emphasize biblical history and its reliability. Some liberal critical theories of the Old Testament that have compromised this reliability include the documentary hypothesis, multiple theories of authorship for Isaiah, and general denial of predictive prophecy in various books, especially Daniel. The New Testament has also seen attacks by radical scholars on its reliability. Many of these make yearly headlines in newspapers and magazines. The apologist and history teacher can incorporate these instances into their lessons to demonstrate the faulty naturalistic assumptions of such attacks and study evidence for the reliability of the biblical text. The defense of the knowability of history as well as presuppositions and principles governing inquiry into lower and higher criticism will benefit both subjects.

Bible and Theology. Students usually will take Bible courses before a full apologetics course. Yet, aspects of both can be incorporated even before a systematic and distinct apologetics course is taken. In many cases, the Bible teacher may also be the apologetics teacher and usually has a strong background in biblical and theological studies. However, apologetics should serve a direct foundational role for Bible and theological studies. For theology, apologetics demonstrates that the Bible is the word of God and as such must be inerrant. This area is known as prolegomena and begins the task of arguing that the inerrancy of Scripture is the foundation upon which evangelical theology is built. Theology, then must take from philosophical arguments to show that contrary theological approaches are wrong. For example, some theologies deny the classical attributes of God. Theology must use the same rational arguments of natural theology, to demonstrate the truth of these attributes. Other areas needing a similar type of support include the adequacy of meaning human language to express truth about God.[11] While some of these areas

10. See Hagopian, *The Genesis Debate.* Two ministries representing each major view include Reasons to Believe www.reasons.org (progressive creationism) and Institute for Creation Research www.icr.org (young earth creationism).

11. See Geisler, *Introduction Bible.*

are quite technical and involved, some level of discussion and awareness is possible for the beginning apologetic and theology student.

For biblical studies, apologetics can help in the study of difficult passages that seem even to conflict. A few major works express not only answers to such questions and problems but principles that should be employed when investigating such passages.[12] The student should be aware of such passages, the resources to help solve them, as well as some practice answering difficulties in the Bible.

The interdisciplinary nature of apologetics should not necessarily be limited to only these subjects. Other classes in the humanities and fine arts may have instance of incorporating issues in apologetics. The following chart shows areas where these major subjects have material corresponding to the unit in apologetics.

Unit	Reading	Writing	Mathematics	Communication (Oral)	Philosophy	Science	History	Bible & Theology
1-A	X	X		X	X		X	X
1-B	X	X		X	X			X
2-A	X	X		X	X			X
2-B	X	X		X	X			X
2-C	X	X		X	X			X
2-D	X	X		X	X	X	X	X
3-A	X	X	X	X	X		X	X
3-B	X	X		X	X		X	X
3-C	X	X		X	X			X
3-D	X	X		X	X	X	X	X
3-E	X	X	X	X	X	X	X	X
3-F	X	X		X	X			X
3-G	X	X		X	X			X

Table 8.2 Basic Interdisciplinary Skills Chart

12. Geisler and Howe, *When Critics Ask*.

Delivery of Information and Instructional Evaluation

What may an apologetics class involve as far as how content is delivered to secondary student? While methods and techniques may greatly differ depending on teacher style and student abilities (including different learning styles), I would like to suggest some methods that are likely to be used and indicate what a curriculum should include to facilitate these methods.

Audiovisual methods. The most popular and often used method to deliver apologetics is lecturing (either with or without visual images). In the secondary class room, however, the effectiveness of this method alone must be evaluated. The secondary student attention span is not that of an adult and this may be one of the most ineffective methods. This is especially the case given that this is usually their first exposure to the subject and at times higher level abstract thinking is needed. My classroom experience has caused me to keep the pure lecture method to no longer than 15 minutes (or one quarter of the total allotted teaching period). Giving students immediate visual reinforcement of content and concepts presented in the lecture is also imperative. This can be accomplished through electronic software media or hardcopy handouts. Both should be facilitated by the curriculum. These may include cartoons, charts, collages, demonstrations, diagrams, displays, exhibits, drawings, field trips, movie clips, interviews, music, object lessons, outlines, photographs (slide shows), timelines, etc.

Discussion methods. Once audiovisual content is delivered discussion methods can be effective in reinforcing apologetics content that has been delivered. Having students use and do apologetics activities not only reinforce learning, it is a good way for the teacher to evaluate the effectiveness of audiovisual delivery methods. Students can prepare and engage in mini or long debates, question and answer sessions, group brainstorming, case studies, forums, guided discussions, interviews, panel discussions, speeches, workshops, etc. Putting the student in the position where they must use, communicate and teach others apologetics is an important completion to the cycle of learning.

Dramatic methods. A creative outlet for apologetics can involve the dramatic presentation of apologetics. These may involve dialogues, dramatic reading, monologues, role playing, skits, TV or radio programs.

Project methods. Working on projects, having something tangible at the end, is a good way to help students to see and feel that they have truly accomplished something with their understanding of apologetics. Beyond the assignment/homework normally given, the student can engage in special projects that involve case studies of groups or individuals especially of those needing apologetics, write and print apologetics newsletters, reports, and interviews, develop and use surveys or questionnaires, develop and play apologetic games, puzzles, etc.

As students progress in their apologetic abilities, these methods, as much as possible, should involve people and groups outside the classroom either as participants or observers/learners. A curriculum should suggest different methods and activities that may be relevant to certain areas of apologetics. The methods may vary, grow and adapt over time, but evaluation of these methods and student learning is essential to measuring effectiveness. Answers to such questions as (1) did the method accomplish the lesson objective? (2) Did the method meet student needs? (3) Did the method encourage student participation in apologetics? (4) How did students change in attitude/behavior towards apologetics? (5) Did students retain apologetics information or arguments? And (6) did students grow in apologetic abilities or capacities? Answers to these kinds of questions will help an apologetics teacher improve and change to more effective teaching methods.

Selecting and Using Apologetics Curriculum

One of the most important things I have ever discovered regarding curriculum is that "*the teacher is the curriculum.*"[13] Once that door shuts and the teacher starts to teach, everything else you have done diminishes in importance. However, there are some important things to be aware of when it comes to developing or choosing a curriculum. A professor in my curriculum class once said, "When it comes to teachers developing curriculum, there are those that can and those that can't." Some teachers excel in the development phase of teaching. They work well behind the scenes in preparing what to teach and when. Others excel at the delivery phase. They work best when actually teaching and especially performing the lesson in the class. It is rare to find those that can do both really well. Some teachers love to teach and others love to prepare to teach. Even if they can do both the problem of finding time to do both well is sometimes difficult. As apologetics education at the secondary level

---

13. Senter, "Principles of Leadership Recruitment," 469.

expands, more curriculums of a professionally published nature may follow. Hence, I would like to give some practical advice in selecting and using an apologetics curriculum.

There are some crucial areas from which to ask questions that will help you select and perhaps develop your own curriculum. The first area of the importance is that the curriculum matches classical apologetics, and age level of the students. If you develop or adapt a curriculum to meet your needs, it becomes important to make sure nothing violates that methodology and that you have a good assessment of the level and ability of your students.

Second, theological and doctrinal considerations are important. To be more precise you will want not only to look for what is heretical (directly contrary to orthodoxy), but to things that are aberrant (off base), sub-orthodox (less then orthodoxy), and heterodoxy (differing from orthodoxy).[14] It is very easy for subtle statements and suggestions to creep in and jeopardize doctrinal integrity. A curriculum reviewer or teacher should constantly be on the guard for any statements or hints directly or indirectly that maybe suspicious, if not directly heretical. The publisher or author may not even knowingly have suggesting something contrary to evangelical theology. They may not even be directly written, non-evangelical theologies and theologies that are even more radical can easily creep into presuppositions, illustrations and figures. Such influences are bound to surface, even in secondary school curriculum. There are many controversies even in the evangelical community that may influence curriculum development. The teacher or director cannot let their guard down. If something is found, even after you have implemented use of the curriculum materials in a class, take the opportunity to create a learning situation and discuss the problem with your class. It can become an opportunity to expose the *subtleties* of theological error.

Third, you must review the substance and organization of the curriculum material. The goals should be stated in measurable terms of the student. The supporting materials must meet the objectives and goals. They should be significant objectives and the material should flow and develop in a logical and systematic order. If the two do not match, then it is probably in need of significant changes and revision. There is no use stating objectives that are not achievable through instruction or giving instruction for objectives that are not measurable.

14. See Bowman, *Orthodoxy and Heresy*.

Fourth, the curriculum should facilitate teaching and learning. There should be a wide variety of teaching techniques and materials for the teacher to use and adapt. Not all teachers teach the same and not all learners learn the same. A variety is essential for both teaching and learning to be successful. It must also help the teacher and learner integrate the spiritual maturity and aid the student in developing a personal relationship with Jesus Christ and give opportunities for experiences that build maturity concerning the subject during the teaching-learning process.

Finally, once a curriculum is decided upon and implemented it should undergo an evaluation during and after it has been implemented. One important model of evaluation is that provided by the late professor Doris A Freese. There she identifies various stages of an educational cycle which involves developing, implementing, administrative, delivering, evaluating, and revising an educational program.[15] Any educational program, including an apologetics one, should undergo this type of evaluative process to increase its effectiveness.

We have laid out the necessary parts of a curriculum on apologetics that are needed to assist the teacher. These include a rational for teaching apologetics, general and specific objectives for each unit, activities and instructional aids, evaluation and discussed the importance of integrating apologetics with other subjects.

QUESTIONS TO ANSWER

1. What are some specific goals and objectives for teaching apologetics in your educational setting?

2. Choose a subject to integrate into an apologetics class and develop some specific goals or objectives.

3. What should be included in a successful apologetics curriculum?

SELECT READINGS

Lawrence O. Richards and Gary J. Bredfeldt, *Creative Bible Teaching.*
Roy B. Zuck, *Teaching as Jesus Taught.*

---

15. Freese with Brubaker, "The Church's Educational Ministry," Clark, *Christian Education*, 395–410.

9

The Future of Christian Apologetics Education

OBJECTIVES

*Assess the present situation concerning Christian
apologetics and the secondary Christian school.*

*Evaluate present and future challenges to Christian
apologetics education at the secondary level.*

OVER THE BRIEF TIME that I have studied apologetics, I have seen
a tremendous growth in the number of published works on the
subject and related areas. Some have even described our time as a re-
naissance in apologetics. I can only assume this represents an increased
interest in the need for the subject. However, not all apologetics are created equally (see chapter 2) and vary not only in their methodology but
also in practice. The trickle down affect of apologetics from the scholarly
ranks has been slow. But many secondary educators and homeschool
teachers are realizing its need and taking steps in the right direction.
When I graduated from college as a new high school teacher, my advisor
required us to buy a 400 plus page curriculum that contained everything
we needed to teach our subject. He explained that when we went out
into the schools one of the first things we would find is that we would
be given so many other duties and responsibilities in the school that we
would have very little time to spend on developing teaching materials
and techniques for use in the classroom. We would need something to
fall back on that could at least provide ideas and suggestions on what
to do in the classroom. He was right! Whether you are a teacher or homeschool parent, you probably understand. The very thing we wish we

could spend most of our time doing, as teachers, ends up being the last thing for which we seem to have time. We may draw upon our memories of what it was like to go through science, math, history, or even Bible classes, or you may pick up the latest teaching methods text on these subjects, but what about apologetics? It is my sincere hope and prayer that what was presented in these pages will be viewed as a start.

Toward that beginning I would like to suggest some areas of study, we did not cover which are nonetheless important for the future of educational apologetics. First, a full apologetic curriculum geared to the secondary school student needs to be developed that is classical and systematic in its approach to apologetics. This should be a curriculum packed with everything a teacher will need to adequately instruct secondary students in the subject of apologetics. I have included a sample unit from such a curriculum in Appendix B to indicate the minimum that such a curriculum should contain. Second, a more complete textbook, specifically geared to the secondary school reader, needs to be written to supplement the curriculum and instruction. Some steps toward a text have been made and even included some evaluation and testing, but there is much room for improvement.[1] Such a work should be developed to meet or exceed the entire criterion suggested in this work (page 121). Third, studies on existing secondary Christian schools to assess the type of courses currently taught on apologetics as well as collecting information related to student achievement are needed. Going to the student, to see if they can adequately defend the faith, after taking an apologetics class, is the only way to measure achievement. Fourth, requirements and qualifications of teachers instructing these courses need to be developed. While some Christian colleges and seminaries are making apologetics a more prominent field of study, this does not necessarily fill the gap of finding teachers qualified at the secondary level of education that can teach apologetics. One can be an excellent apologist, but a poor teacher and the best teachers, do not necessary have the right apologetic approach. Fifth, there is little investigation to see what competencies or lessons would be appropriate in primary or middle school that would advance or anticipate the secondary school student entering a CAE program. Sixth, additional exploration and investigation needs to be done to assess a need for any separate or combined courses in related fields of study such as world religions, cults, the occult, ethics, etc. at the

1. Snuffer, "Truth in Focus."

secondary school level. Additionally, more advanced and basic courses and lessons could be developed in these subjects to round out a full curriculum from the primary grades to the secondary. I am aware of a few teachers that have developed curriculum in these related areas and it is not beyond the realm of having to incorporate these areas of study into an overall education curriculum on apologetics.[2] Also nothing seems to be available which helps prepares educators and missionaries to teach across-cultures apologetics education at the secondary level. Finally, in general, there are few articles or studies written that assess or identify specific or special needs of students related to an apologetics course of study at the secondary school level. Additional work in all of these areas would advance the justification and implementation of apologetics at the secondary school level.

I do hope and pray the future will see every secondary student taking a class, in the tradition of classical apologetics, similar to the one described in this book, as a part of Christian home and institutional school education. The intellectual and spiritual benefits, indeed, may be far reaching. Think about it. Every Christian high school graduate may be as knowledgeable about apologetics as they are math, science, English, history or any other subject taught at the secondary level. Such individuals will at least be equipped in basics apologetics and may become life long learners of the subject. Christian adults of every occupation may recall the proper method and content of defending the Christian faith and incorporate such into their thinking, living, and learning. Our world has yet to see an army of life-long learning apologists, apart from professionals, who will go forth thinking and speaking intelligently about their Christian faith, and most importantly able to give an answer when needed to help advance the gospel of Jesus Christ.

QUESTIONS TO ANSWER

1. What do you think will be the most significant challenges to Christian apologetics education in the future?

2. What should Christian educators do to open further the door for apologetics at the secondary school level?

2. Toenges, "World Religions and Cults"; Pietruski, "Comparing Orthodox Christian Doctrine with Select Major Cults"; and Rodriguez, "Wise as Serpents-Harmless as Doves."

3. What steps can you take to introduce or improve a Christian apologetics educational program at your school?

SELECT READINGS

Avery Dulles, *A History of Apologetics*, chapter 7.

John Stackhouse, *Humble Apologetics*, chapter 11.

J. P. Moreland, *Love Your God with All Your Mind*, chapter 10.

Appendix A

Research on Christian Apologetics Education in the Secondary School

FEW SECONDARY CHRISTIAN EDUCATORS know if, and much less how, other schools are teaching apologetics. The following research attempted to use a descriptive inquiry as to the status of Christian apologetics, as a subject of study, in Christian institutional schools at the secondary level. One of the purposes of this survey is to find out specifically what Christian schools are doing with the subject of Christian apologetics. Are they teaching apologetics; if so, how; under what methodology; and for how long, etc. To that end, we explored the dynamics of this subject in nine related questions:

1. Does your school teach the subject of Christian Apologetics?

2. What grade levels are included in class(es) that have instruction in Christian Apologetics?

3. Does your school teach Christian Apologetics as a distinct subject of study similar to other subjects such as math, science, or Bible?

4. How many weeks of instruction are offered in Christian Apologetics?

5. Do any of your teachers, teaching Christian Apologetics have a degree in the subject such as BA, MA, MDiv, etc. in "Christian Apologetics"?

6. Have any of your teachers ever received formal training in how to teach Christian Apologetics?

7. How would the method of Christian Apologetics offered by your school best be classified?

8. Approximately how many years has your school been teaching Christian Apologetics?

9. What are the textbook(s) or other curriculum materials your school uses for teaching Christian Apologetics?

This descriptive study was conducted in June 2007 under the sponsorship of Southern Evangelical Seminary, Charlotte, North Carolina. I take full responsibility for the development, implementation, and recording of the results. No claim is made to scientific accuracy. Schools were selected if they met the following criteria: They are an accredited[1] Christian secondary school in the United States of America with an e-mail address. The first request for completion of the survey was sent via e-mail to 605 secondary Christian schools. Sixty surveys were returned as undeliverable or rejected because the school did not have any secondary Christian students. A second request for completion was made that included 545 surveys. Nine were returned undeliverable or did not include any secondary students. The final count of successful surveys delivered was 536. The first request resulted in thirty-seven usable surveys. For the second request, thirty-three usable surveys were returned. The total usable surveys returned were seventy. Which resulted in a 13 percent return rate. Twenty-six states are represented in the returned sample the most being from Texas, California, Virginia, and Ohio. The estimate of the total number of students attending the represented schools in the returned surveys is 15,913. This figure is based on the number reported in the survey by the responders. In what follows, we will discuss some of the assumptions, value, strengths, weakness, and results of each question.

TEACHING THE SUBJECT OF CHRISTIAN APOLOGETICS

It is assumed the responder understands what the subject means and whether or not it is taught in their school. In the e-mail message, receivers were asked if they did not feel qualified to answer the questions, to forward the message to another person that they thought would be better qualified. This question was introductory and simple, yet important to establish an understanding of the nature of the survey. It is broad enough to cover structured as well as perhaps less structured learning

---

1. Usually by a regional secondary accrediting agency or the Association of Christian Schools International (ACSI).

situations. However, while some may have thought of such events as chapels including apologetics the term "teach" should have at least limited the responders to official school sponsored instruction whether it was "formalized instruction" or not. There were no missed or unanswered responses to this question. Of those that responded 80 percent said yes, 18 percent responded no, and 1 percent was undecided. It is clear from the results that not every accredited Christian secondary school had decided, in what ever form, to include the subject of Christian apologetics in their teaching. Nonetheless, the vast majority of responding accredited Christian schools do "teach" Christian apologetics.

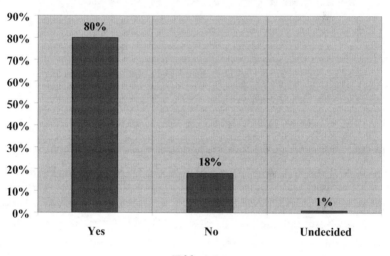

Table A.1

GRADE LEVELS OF INSTRUCTION
IN CHRISTIAN APOLOGETICS

This open ended question listed the levels sixth through twelfth grade. This allowed the responder to select any or all that applied. Hence, the responders were varied and came in the following groups and classifications represented in Table 2. No grade below seven was included in the responses and grades 11–12 received the highest responses of 21 percent. Seventeen percent did not answer the question (N/A). The next highest response was the listing of the individual grades 11 or 12 for teaching apologetics.

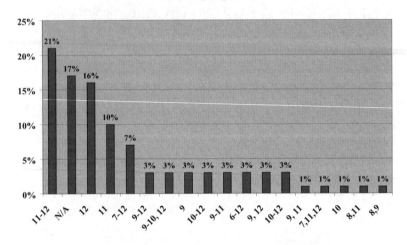

Table A.2

CHRISTIAN APOLOGETICS
AS A DISTINCT SUBJECT OF STUDY

This question persuaded the responder to make a distinction in their apologetic program: Either they integrate the subject into others or they teach it as a separate subject. While it may be that some do both, that option was not available in the answer. It is an assumption that if the school did both they should have answered that they teach it as a distinct subject. Responses to this question were almost evenly split with only a difference of six percentage points. Of those responding, 53 percent do not teach apologetics as a distinct subject and 47 percent of schools said they do teach it as a distinct subject similar to other subjects (Table 3). Since this question was so important to apologetics and how it is taught, the responders answer in the affirmative, were separated to discover how their answers to the various questions differed. For example, a little over half, 51 percent, of those that responded do teach apologetics as a separate subject and they do so at the 11–12 or 12 level alone (Table 4).

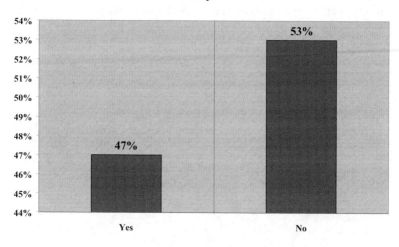

Table A.3

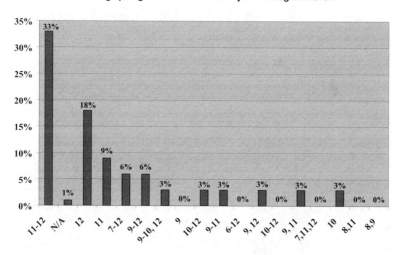

Table A.4

LENGTH OF INSTRUCTION OFFERED
IN CHRISTIAN APOLOGETICS

This open ended question revealed how much time, whether the school integrated or separated the subject, was spent teaching apologetics.

While a significant number provided no answer (N/A) to this question, the majority provide eighteen or thirty-six weeks of integrated or separated instruction in apologetics (Table 5). Of those that separate instruction in apologetics, 39 percent do so for eighteen weeks and 33 percent do so for thirty-six weeks (Table 6).

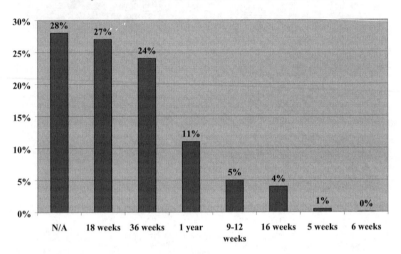

Table A.5

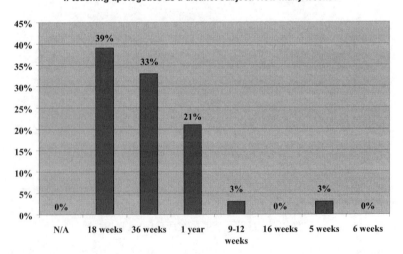

Table A.6

TEACHERS WITH A DEGREE IN THE SUBJECT

This, admittedly, is perhaps the most misunderstood question of the survey. From the responses given, it was not clear to the reader if the question is asking if teachers have a degree in Christian apologetics or if they just have one of the degrees listed. This may be due to the fact that few degrees directly are offered from undergraduate or graduate schools with a major or concentration in the subject of apologetics. Hence, some may have assumed the question was only concerned with the issue of a degree and not the subject or emphasis of that degree. Many may have answered the question in the affirmative if their teacher just had a degree that was similar to the examples (BA, MA, MDiv). Regardless of confusion over the question, the results from responders stated that 66 percent did have such a degree and 28 percent did not (Table 7). When schools that teach apologetics as a separate subject are considered 40 percent have the degree while 60 percent do not (Table 8).

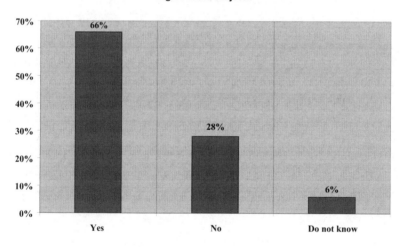

Do any of your teachers, teaching Christian apologetics, have a degree in the subject?

Table A.7

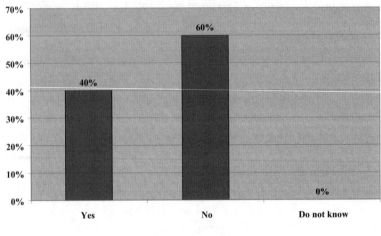

Table A.8

TEACHER TRAINING IN CHRISTIAN APOLOGETICS

This question inquired into the existence of any training for the apologetics teacher. The training should be formalized as opposed to informal or self-taught. It should be in how to teach apologetics and not just how to do apologetics. Such training does not have to be professional and no element of duration, comprehensiveness, or value is suggested by the question. The respondents to the question said 45 percent had received training whereas 21 percent had not. Those that did not know or gave no answer represent 25 percent (Table 9). If the school teaches apologetics as a distinct subject, the number of those that received formal training was 58 percent and 33 percent did not received any training (Table 10).

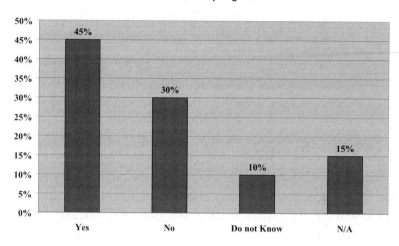

Table A.9

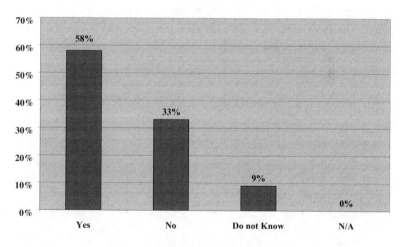

Table A.10

METHOD OF CHRISTIAN APOLOGETICS

Although this question is central to any apologetics educational program, there are some important assumptions built into the question to consider. While most associated with the subject of apologetics realize there are different methods or systems, terminology that describes these different methods is not always agreed upon. The options given were Classical, Evidential, Presuppositional, Reformed (Epistemology), Combinational, Do not know, or other. The terms used were chosen because they are the ones used in two major works on the subject; one an encyclopedia and the other a popular handbook (see Baker *Encyclopedia of Christian Apologetics* and *Faith has its Reasons*). It was believed that most, associated with the field, would at least know what the terms were referring to even if they held differing opinions on their use. The terms, for the most part, are mutually exclusive. If responders checked more than one then they were classified as combinational. This is because the combinational takes the approach of selecting a method that is dependent on the needs of a person or issue. It ignores any conflict with another apologetic method and adapts the other methods as needed. The majority of responders, 38 percent, declared themselves to be combinational in their approach to apologetics. Those that did not know totaled 18 percent and those that did not answer were 15 percent. Classical apologetics tied with the selection of other approaches (which mostly went unspecified) at 7 percent (Table 11). Of the schools teaching apologetics as a distinct subject of study, the majority of them at 54 percent are combinational. The classical method makes up 9 percent, which is equal with those that do not know or describe their method as "other" (Table 12).

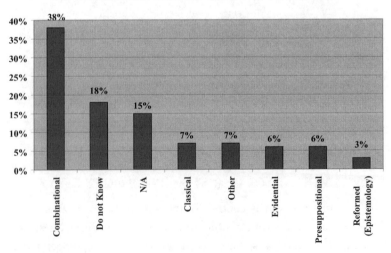

How would the method of Christian apologetics best be classified?

Table A.11

If teaching apologetics as a distinct subject: What is the method?

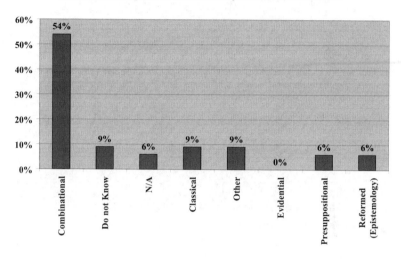

Table A.12

YEARS TEACHING CHRISTIAN APOLOGETICS

The responses concerning the length of time apologetics had been taught as integrated or distinct subject were grouped between four years or less, five-to-nine years, ten years or more. Just more than half of the responding schools, 51 percent have taught Christian apologetics for nine years or less. Twenty-three percent have taught for four years or less and 28 percent have taught between five-to-nine years. Twenty-three percent of responding schools have taught apologetics for ten years or more. Over 20 percent of the schools did not or were not able to answer the question (Table 13). When schools that teach apologetics as a distinct subject are considered alone, 36 percent have done so for four years or less and 30 percent have done so between five-to-nine years. Twenty-two percent have taught for ten years or more (Table 14). However, it should be understood that the schools were not asked when or if they have taught apologetics as a distinct subject for that same duration of time nor were they asked about the method of apologetics used during that duration.

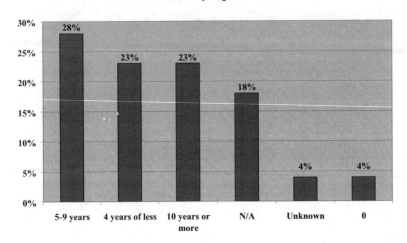

Table A.13

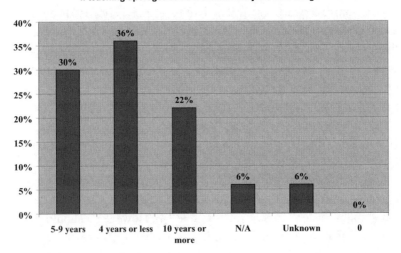

Table A.14

CURRICULUM MATERIALS USED FOR CHRISTIAN APOLOGETICS

This open-ended question attempted to discover what curriculum resources schools are using to teach apologetics. Because of the open-ended nature of the question, the results are simply listed with the frequency the item was listed. The reader should not take this listing of resource or its frequency as an endorsement of its content (in part or in whole) on behalf of the researcher, sponsor, or publisher of this book. Although the responders listed their resources in combinations, these are not revealed in the table. The first column lists the title of the material followed with either the author or publisher in parenthesis if known. The next column is the frequencies for all responders. Frequency is simply the number of times the resource was listed by a responder. The last column shows the frequencies for only responders who indicated that they teach apologetics as a distinct subject of study (Table 15).

Title (Author or Publisher)	Total Frequency	Distinct Subject Frequency
N/A (No Answer)	16	4
Understanding the Times (Noebel)	15	9
The Case for Christ (Strobel)	9	6
Own Material	9	9
Mere Christianity (C. S. Lewis)	5	3
Exploring Apologetics (CIS)	4	4
Universe Next Door (Sire)	4	2
The Case for Faith (Strobel)	3	3
Charts on Christian Apologetics (House)	3	1
Focus on the Family Truth Project	3	0
Christian Apologetic Handbook (Kreeft)	3	0
Living Loud (Geisler) Truth Quest Series	3	2
The Case for a Creator (Strobel)	3	3
More Than a Carpenter (McDowell)	2	2
Timeless Truth (ACSI)	2	2
Unshakable Foundations (Geisler)	2	2
12 Points that Prove Christianity is True (Geisler)	2	2
Summit Ministries	2	0
Thinking Like A Christian (Noebel)	2	2
The Fallacy Detective (Bluedorn)	2	2
I Don't Have Enough Faith to be An Atheist (Geisler)	2	2
Quick Source Guide to Christian Apologetics (Powell)	2	1
Truth in Focus (Snuffer)	1	1
Christianity in Today's Culture (Colson)	1	1
Total Truth (Pearcey)	1	1
Reasonable Faith (Craig)	1	0
5 Minute Apologist (Cornish)	1	0
Pop Goes Religion (Mattingly)	1	1
Know Why You Believe (Little)	2	2
Evidence That Demands a Verdict (McDowell)	1	1
Defending Your Faith (Story)	1	1
Unknown	1	0
The Deadliest Monster (Baldwin)	1	0
Paul Pyle's Biblical Studies Curriculum	1	0
A Ready Defense (McDowell)	1	0
Resurrection Factor (McDowell)	1	0
Reason to Believe (Sproul)	1	0
Abeka Bible Curriculum	1	0
Relativism (Beckwith)	1	1
Rose Publishing Charts	1	1
Skeptics Answered (Kennedy)	1	1
Knowing God (Packer)	1	1
The Pursuit of Godliness (Tozer)	1	1
ACSI Curriculum	1	1

Table A.15

LIMITATIONS AND CONCLUSIONS OF THE STUDY

There are some limitations to consider regarding this study. First, an e-mail based survey assumes the technical ability and desire to receive and return the instrument. Although specific directions were given in the message, as to how to complete and send the survey back. Those without the know-how, desire, or technical ability may have chosen not to participate. Others may never participate in such kinds of surveys. This may have affected the return rate. Yet, similar problems exist with any kind of descriptive survey. Second, as noted above some questions may have been misunderstood. This may have affected some results, especially number five. Third, the nature of the survey itself, all dealing with apologetic questions, may have communicated the expectation that apologetics should be taught at their school. This may or may not have influenced those that answered one way or another. But since a smaller number of responders indicated they did not teach apologetics in any form this either indicates that apologetics is taught in the majority of Christian schools (as indicated by the survey) or the survey itself drove some or many of those that do not teach apologetics away from even responding. This, at worst, would limit the survey to only describing what schools teaching apologetics are in fact doing. Finally, it is important to note that none of these results include apologetics related to non-accredited Christian secondary schools or the homeschool environment.

Even with these limitations considered there are some positive features of this descriptive survey. Over ten percent of the sample audience responded to the survey. Most questions were understood which is evident from the responders who provide clear and quantifiable answers. If the sample is taken to even be somewhat representative of the whole then it is possible to suggest an answer to the question, what are most schools doing concerning apologetics? According to the survey results, most accredited Christian schools in the United States are teaching apologetics. Yet, more of these are not teaching it as a distinct or separated subject similar to other subjects. Instead, it is being integrated among other subjects. Schools are teaching apologetics mostly in grades 11–12 (either combined or separated) for at least eighteen or thirty-six weeks of instruction. Their method of apologetics is mostly combinational. Most of these Christian schools have been teaching apologetics for less than nine years. The most frequently cited curriculum resources used for apologetics are *Understanding the Times* (by David Noebel), *The Case for Christ* (by Lee Strobel), or the school has developed their own material.

Appendix B

Sample Unit

INTRODUCTION TO APOLOGETICS
UNIT 1-A

Unit Objective

AFTER COMPLETION OF THIS unit the student should be able to distinguish between the tasks of apologetics, discuss how they relate to apologetics, and utilize apologetics to solve a problem or objection to Christianity.

Specific Objectives

1. Defines Christian Apologetic terms.

2. States self-evident truths.

3. Identifies self-referential statements.

4. Describes the difference between evangelism and pre-evangelism.

5. States and explains important verses on apologetics.

6. Identifies major figures in the history of apologetics.

7. Identifies uses for apologetics in the Community or Church.

8. Discusses how the stages of apologetic reasoning relate.

9. Responds to an apologetic problem in a group setting.

Suggested Resources for this Unit

RECOMMENDED TEXT BOOK

Norman L. Geisler and Ronald M. Brooks. *When Skeptics Ask*, chapter 1.

RECOMMENDED BOOK RESOURCES

Norman L. Geisler and Joseph Holden. *Living Loud: Defending Your Faith*, chapter 1.

Frederic R. Howe, *Challenge and Response: A Handbook of Christian Apologetics*, chapters 1–6.

Josh McDowell. *The New Evidence that Demands a Verdict*, Introduction, part 4.

RECOMMENDED VISUAL AIDS

False Gods of Our Time. Jeremiah Films.

Four 20-minute videos covering three world views (Atheism, Pantheism, and Theism), Creation and basic Apologetics. Available from: www.jeremiahfilms.com

Norman Geisler and Frank Turek. *12 Points That Show Christianity is True*. DVD.

Seven hours of video lectures on Christian Apologetics. Available from: www.impactapologetics.com

RECOMMENDED JOURNALS AND MAGAZINES

Christian Research Journal Available from: www.equip.org

Christian Apologetics Journal Available from: www.ses.edu

Journal of the International Society of Christian Apologetics: www.isca -apologetics.org

RECOMMENDED APOLOGETIC MINISTRIES/WEBSITES

http://www.apologeticsgateway.com/

Suggested Activities

A. Obtain additional materials and/or invite resource people to class to supplement/reinforce information provided in this unit of instruction.

B. Make transparencies from the transparency masters or use the digital files included with this unit.

C. Provide students with objective sheet.

D. Discuss Unit and Specific objectives.

E. Provide students with information and assignment sheets.

F. Discuss information and assignment sheets.

G. Integrate the following activities throughout the teaching of this unit.

    1. Use the Types of Apologetics as a model of how to organize and address apologetic questions and objections. Any question or objection to Christianity can be placed into one of these areas. Examine what must be true prior to examining the question or objection.

    2. Sometimes there are conferences or seminars held on apologetics in various local churches. These would be an excellent opportunity for students and teachers to receive further information and training in apologetics.

    3. Show videos introducing students to apologetics and related ministries.

    4. Discuss the historical development of apologetics by developing a timeline with photos of apologists, dates, books, and significant issues.

    5. Discuss how apologetics changed your thinking about your faith and life with your students.

    6. Give examples or illustrations of apologetics being used in pre-evangelism.

    7. Discuss problems and concerns related to doing apologetics.

    8. Use and incorporate the Appendix in the text "An argument for Christianity" with each unit as a preview, review, and map for the overall content of the course and apologetic for Christianity.

H. Use the activity sheets or develop other activities to do with students.

I. Administer tests.

J. Evaluate tests.

K. Re-teach if necessary.

INTRODUCTION TO APOLOGETICS
UNIT 1-A

Information Sheet

A.   WHAT IS APOLOGETICS?

1. Terms and Definitions

Apologetics—The application of knowledge to demonstrate that Christianity is true.

Philosophy—The love and pursuit of knowledge, beauty, and truth.

Logic—The study of right reason and valid argumentation.

Argument—Providing a reason for the basis of a conclusion.

Truth—That which corresponds to reality.

Self-evident truth—Something that is intuitively true and cannot be denied (for example, "I exist" cannot be denied)

Theism—The belief that one transcendent (separate Being from the Universe) God exists.

Bible—The collection of 66 ancient books written under divine inspiration.

Faith—Believing something is true based upon the authority of another.

Ethics—The study of that which is morally right and wrong.

Evangelism—Explaining to another the New Testament gospel of Jesus Christ.

2. Three tasks of apologetics.

```
┌─────────────────────────────────────┐
│        TRUTH OF CHRISTIANITY         │
│         QUESTIONS ABOUT . . .        │
│       BIBLE    JESUS CHRIST          │
├─────────────────────────────────────┤
│          EXISTENCE OF GOD            │
│         QUESTIONS ABOUT . . .        │
│  GOD  MIRACLES  EVIL  WORLD VIEW     │
├─────────────────────────────────────┤
│       PHILOSOPHICAL FOUNDATION       │
│         QUESTIONS ABOUT . . .        │
│  TRUTH  KNOWLEDGE  SELF-EVIDENT      │
│                        TRUTH         │
└─────────────────────────────────────┘
```

Philosophical Foundation: Answers basic questions such as what is truth? What is knowledge? Is anything absolutely true?

Existence of God: Uses arguments to show that God exists and answers questions concerning evil and miracles.

Truth of Christianity: Uses historical arguments to show the Bible is reliable and Jesus rose from the dead.

3. Relationship of the three tasks of apologetics.

Truth is the foundation to apologetic reasoning.

If truth is possible, then it is possible to give a true argument for the existence of God.

If God exists, then it is possible to argue that the Bible is His Word.

You must know what kind of question is asked in order to develop a correct answer.

It makes no sense to argue that the Bible is the Word of God (Truth of Christianity) if the person does not believe there is a God (Existence of God)

B.   THE USE OF APOLOGETICS (CHAPTER 1)

1. Evangelism—is giving the gospel or good news about Jesus Christ.

2. Pre-Evangelism—is giving reasons for your faith. It is done only when an objection or question is raised.

3. Giving the answer—There are good reasonable answers to give unbelievers about the Christian faith.

    a. Apologetics can be . . .

        1) Negative—arguing that another position is not true.

        2) Positive—arguing that Christianity is true.

    b. Should be based on reason and seek to clarify Christian teaching.

4. Biblical precedence—The Bible commands us to be ready to give an answer concerning our faith.

    a. 1 Peter 3:15

    b. 2 Cor 10:5

    c. Jude 3

    d. Titus 1:9

    e. 2 Tim 2:24–25

5. Answering Objections to Apologetics

    a. Prov. 26:4 says "do not answer a fool according to his folly."

        1) Verse 5 says answer a fool as his folly deserves.

        2) The lesson is to not argue with someone who will not listen to reason.

    b. Logic cannot tell us anything about God

        1) Statement is self-defeating or violates the law of non-contradictions.

        2) Logic is a valid tool for discovering truth.

        3) When a truth cannot be denied, it must be true.

   c. Pre-evangelism or apologetics is not in the Bible

      1) Moses did pre-evangelism by confronting mythical accounts of creation with the true account of creation.

      2) Elijah did pre-evangelism by challenging the prophets of Baal on Mount Carmel.

      3) Jesus did apologetics by confronting the Pharisees of his day with his divinity.

  C. Supplemental Reading on History of Apologetics. (Note: It is not necessary to teach the classifications of apologetics at this point).

New Testament, (50–90 AD)

BACKGROUND

While no book in the New Testament should be considered a treatise on apologetics, it is replete with instances of apologetic activity. There are obvious places where writers answered questions and objections about the faith, described apologetic activity, and encouraged us to defend the faith. Much of the New Testament apologetic concerns itself with the historical foundation of Christianity, warnings about false teachers, and a defense of the gospel. Some of the most obvious New Testament apologetics are found in the writings of Luke, John, Peter, and Paul.

APOLOGETICS

Jesus, as portrayed in the Gospels, uses many conflicts with the Jewish leaders to present an apologetic for himself (Matt 22:41–46). He also warns his followers against false teachers (Matt 7:15–20). Luke begins his Gospel by citing the careful extent he has gone to in order to write about Jesus (Luke 1:1–3). He goes on to use the speeches of the apostles as apologetics to both Jews and Gentiles. The first time the gospel of Christ's death and resurrection is preached, it is defended. Peter, as recorded by Luke, presents the gospel and defends it by citing prophetic statements from the Old Testament (Acts 2). The Apostle Paul debated regularly with Jews in the synagogues and on one occasion, the nature of God and the resurrection with Greek philosophers (Acts 17). Peter encourages Christians to "give a defense to everyone that asks . . ." (1 Pet 3:15) and Jude exhorts us to "contend earnestly for the faith . . ." (Jude 3).

SIGNIFICANT WORKS
> Luke: Gospel of Luke and Acts;
> John: Gospel of John;
> Paul: 1–2 Corinthians, Romans, Galatians, Colossians;
> Peter: 1–2 Peter;
> Hebrews.

Paul/Saul, (1–10–65/67 AD)

BACKGROUND

Paul, formally known as Saul, was born in Tarsus sometime in the first decade of the Christian era. He was born a Jew of the tribe of Benjamin but also had the privilege of Roman citizenship. Around the age of thirteen, he was sent to Jerusalem to study. Eventually he studied under Gamaliel and became a Pharisee equally fluent in Aramaic and Greek. Upon seeing the risen Christ on the road to Damascus, he was converted to Christianity (33) and spent his early years as a believer in Syria, Arabia, and Judea. Later he embarked on three missionary journeys where he started, visited, and wrote letters to churches. He was placed under house arrest in Rome and according to tradition was beheaded as a martyr (65–67).

APOLOGETICS

Luke records many of Paul's speeches, called apologies, before officials (Acts 22:1; 24:10; 25:8; 26:1, 24). Paul makes an apologetic to challenges that came from three main groups: Jews, Pagans, and Gnostics. Paul's custom after entering a city was to go to the synagogue to reason from the Scriptures with the Jews. Paul would defend Jesus as the Messiah that died and rose from the dead. He would prove this from the Old Testament predictions fulfilled in the life of Jesus. He also defended the gospel from the attack of Judaizers who added works to salvation (Galatians 3). Against Paganism, Paul argued in the Athenian marketplace and before a group of philosophers known as the Areopagus. There, he defended God's nature and the approval of Jesus demonstrated by his resurrection. An early form of Gnosticism that attacked the deity of Jesus and taught strange beliefs caused Paul to write in defense of the faith to Colossians.

SIGNIFICANT WORKS
Galatians;
1–2 Corinthians;
Romans;
Colossians.

Justin Martyr, (100–165 AD)

BACKGROUND
Justin Martyr was of Greek descent and a native of Samaria, city of Flvia Neapolis. He was well educated in several philosophy systems. He was converted to Christianity after meeting a Christian that used arguments to show that Platonism was inconsistent. After his conversion, he taught in Asia Minor and Rome at private Christian schools. Eventually, along with six others, Justine was brought to trial and charged with being a Christian. He admitted to the charge and was scourged and beheaded.

CLASSIFICATION
Reactionary Apologetics

APOLOGETICS
In his works, Justin addresses a number of issues related to apologetics. One of the first charges leveled against Christians was their refusal to worship the many gods (polytheism) of the established government. Because of this, Christians were charged with what was perceived to be Atheism (belief in no God). He answered that the charge is true as far as 'gods' are concerned, but false when it comes to the 'true God.' Justin addressed and answered the prevalent problem of idol worship. He considered them not only senseless, but insulting to God. Justin also contended for the reasonableness of a future resurrection for believers. Against paganism, Justin argued for the truth of Christianity by citing prophecies from the Old Testament.

SIGNIFICANT WORKS
First Apology (150–60);
Second Apology (150–60).

Origen, (185–253 AD)

BACKGROUND

As a child, Origen fled the city of Alexandria because Christians were being persecuted. His father was martyred because of persecution and a wealthy woman took Origen in to raise him. At the age of eighteen, he was chosen to fill the headmaster position at a Christian school. He eventually returned to Alexandria but then shortly moved to Palestine where he lived out the rest of his life. He was tortured under Emperor Decius for his faith and eventually died (253).

CLASSIFICATION

Reactionary Apologetics

APOLOGETICS

Origen was probably one of the most prolific Christian writers of ancient times. Although he adopted a number of heretical beliefs, he provided one of the strongest early defenses of Christianity. He argued against Celsus (177–180AD) a Jew who was by far the most significant intellectual antagonist of Christian thought up to this time. Origen answered the charge of Celsus that Jesus practiced sorcery, that Jesus could not be God, and that the accounts of his death and resurrection were a myth or a trick. Origen responded confidently to these charges point by point. Even today, modern apologists use some of Origen's arguments and points.

SIGNIFICANT WORK

Against Celsus (178).

Aurelius Augustine, (354–430 AD)

BACKGROUND

Augustine was born in the home of a Roman official in Tagast, a North African town. His mother was Monica who prayed for his conversion to Christianity. Prior to his conversion, Augustine was involved in a cult known as Manicheism. He was converted to Christianity in 386 after meditating on his spiritual need and reading Romans 13:13–14 in a garden. He was educated in a local school and then was sent off to school in Madaura and later Carthage. He was ordained as a priest in 391 and became bishop of Hippo in 396. By the end of his life he had written over one hundred books, five hundred sermons and two hundred letters. These works covered a wide range of topics about human culture, theology, philosophy, and history.

CLASSIFICATION
Classical Apologetics

APOLOGETICS
Augustine's early apologetics refuted the Manicheism cult that believed good and evil are equals. As he matured in his theology, he wrote many works against paganism, heresies, and developed a more complete Christian world view. He believed that faith and reason were interactive in coming to know God through Jesus Christ. Augustine cited Romans 1:20 to show that pagans had knowledge of God. He used arguments for the existence of God, proofs of fulfilled prophecy, miracles in the Bible, and the spread of Christianity to convince unbelievers that Christianity is true.

SIGNIFICANT WORKS
Confessions (401) gives a spiritual autobiography;
Against the Academics (386) is his most philosophical work;
The Enchiridion (421) concerns his theological views;
The City of God (413–26) is his greatest apologetic work.

Anselm, (1033–1109 AD)

BACKGROUND
Anselm was born in Aosta, in northern Italy and around 1056 came to a monastery called Bec in Normandy. He eventually was nominated to archbishop of Canterbury in 1093 and served for sixteen years. He gained a reputation for a strong mixture of piety and great intellectual powers. Plato (428–348 BC), an ancient Greek philosopher, and Augustine were significant influences on his thought. His most original work in Apologetics concerns an argument for the existence of God. This controversial and enduring argument known as the Ontological (argument from being or existence) is still debated today.

CLASSIFICATION
Classical Apologetics

APOLOGETICS

Anselm believed similar to Augustine that faith and reason were complimentary. He understood reason to help believers have assurance and prepare them to give others an answer. He defended the Deity of Jesus Christ and the Trinity. He argued and believed that both were reasonable. He defended the nature of truth and the existence of God. Truth he defined as that which corresponds to reality. The Cosmological argument was based on God's goodness and his Ontological argument uses the idea of a necessary being (a being that must exist) to an existing necessary being that is God. He believed historical evidence and miracles supported the truth of Christianity.

SIGNIFICANT WORK

> *Monologion* develops a cosmological type argument
> for God's existence;
> *Proslogion* develops the ontological argument for God's existence;
> *Cur Deus Homo* argues for the Deity of Jesus Christ;
> *Truth* defends the correspondence nature of truth.

Thomas Aquinas, (1224/5–1274 AD)

BACKGROUND

Thomas was born to a noble family in the town of Aquinas, Italy. He was dedicated by his parents to the Benedictine order at the school in Monte Cassino. He eventually became a Dominican monk and studied under Albert the Great in Paris. Albert moved to Cologne and Aquinas followed him to continue his studies. Aquinas received the Master of Theology in 1256 and continued to teach in Paris and Italy until his death. Aquinas was a theologian and philosopher who wrote on many issues. He authored over one hundred books including commentaries on both the Old and New Testament. He was greatly influenced by the Greek philosopher Aristotle. His greatest work, the *Summa Theologiae*, attempts to cover all areas of theology. It contains three thousand articles and answers six hundred questions. The work, as large as it is, was never completely finished. Aquinas was a great analytic thinker and his writing style is sometimes very complex.

CLASSIFICATION

Classical Apologetics

APOLOGETICS

Aquinas believed that God has revealed himself in nature and Scripture. Nature or General revelation reveals God's attributes and is available to everyone. Scripture or Special revelation reveals doctrines that could not be discovered by human reason such as the Trinity. Concerning faith and reason, Aquinas made the distinction between belief (or faith) *in* and belief *that*. God's existence can be proved by human reason, but should never be the basis for faith *in* God. One can believe that God exists by human reasoning, but should never be the basis for believing *in* God. He demonstrated God's existence in five ways 1) from motion to an unmoved Mover, 2) from effect to a First Cause, 3) from contingent being to a Necessary Being, 4) from degrees of perfection to a Most Perfect Being, and 5) from design to a Designer. His arguments are based on First Principles that are grounded in reality.

SIGNIFICANT WORK

> *Summa Theologiae* Systematic Theology;
> *Summa contra Gentiles* Apologetic to Islam;
> *On Being and Essence* Philosophical work.

Blaise Pascal (1623–1662)

BACKGROUND

Blaise Pascal was born in France. He was a brilliant mathematician and scientist. Several mathematical proofs and even a scientific law have been named after him. When he was sixteen he completed an original treatise and later made contributions to calculus and mathematical probability. His conversion to Christianity began after he came in contact with a Catholic splinter group called Jansenists. His most significant apologetics work is *Pensées* (which means Thoughts). His apologetic work was often misunderstood and thought to be Fideistic (believing without evidence or proof). However, Pascal was following the tradition laid down by Augustine that used reason in support of Christian faith.

CLASSIFICATION

Evidential Apologetics

Apologetics

Pascal's apologetic can be divided into three parts: evidences, fulfilled prophecies, and his famous 'wager.' His evidences for Christianity included the firmly established facts of Christianity, the miracles of Holy Scripture, and the continuing growth and holiness of the religion. He notes several detailed fulfilled prophecies concerning Jesus' birth and work in Jerusalem. Pascal's Wager argued that either God exists or he does not. If you choose not to believe and he exists, you loose everything. If you believe in him and he does not exist, you loose nothing. So why not believe in him? While this argument fails as a rational proof, it does provide a path of prudence (wisdom).

Significant Work

Pensées a collection of sayings.

Joseph Butler (1692–1752)

Background

Joseph Butler was born in Wantage, England. He was raised as a Presbyterian but converted to the Church of England. He was appointed as a preacher in 1719 in Rolls Chapel in Charcery Lane. Soon he moved on to become Bishop of Bristol and then dean of St. Paul's in 1740. He gained a reputation as a pastoral philosopher because he gave philosophically persuasive arguments with the intent defensively to answer those who wanted to disregard the Christian religion.

Classification

Evidential Apologetics.

Apologetics

Joseph Butler's defense was primarily against Deism. Deism believes that there is a God, but that he does not intervene into the natural course of events in the World. Hence, Deism would reject that there is a revelation from God or that miracles occur. Butler argued by means of an analogy for the truth of Christianity. In essence, he argued that natural religion (Deism) admits similar beliefs as revealed religion (Christianity). Hence, it is not unreasonable to believe in Christianity. Butler further gave arguments for miracles and indicated the inconsistencies in the Deistic position. For example, they believe God created the world (biggest miracle of all), yet reject the possibility of smaller miracles. Why not accept the possibility of smaller miracles if you believe in the largest one? Taken collectively, Butler's apologetic, was quite unified and argued for many aspects of the Christian faith.

SIGNIFICANT WORK

Analogy of Religion (1736) argument against Deism.

William Paley (1743–1805)

BACKGROUND

William Paley was born in Peterborough, England. He graduated from Christ's College, Cambridge, in 1763. His interests were primarily in mathematics, but he accepted a teaching position at Christ College and taught metaphysics, morals, and New Testament Greek. He was ordained as a priest in 1776 and served in several positions in Anglican churches and parishes.

CLASSIFICATION

Classical Apologetics.

APOLOGETICS

Paley's apologetic follows the classical approach of arguing for God and then for Christianity. He authored two books, one titled *Natural Theology* that covers the existence of God and another titled *Evidences* that covers the truth of Christianity. His argument for God is a formulation of the teleological argument. It reasons that if one found a stone and asked how it came to be there, the answer might be that it had just always been. But if one came across a watch, the answer certainly would not be that it has just always been there. A watch, because of its design, needs an intelligent cause as an explanation. This he applied to nature by arguing likewise for one Designer to explain the design uniformity present in all parts of the world. For the evidence of Christianity he appealed to miracles and responded to the famous skeptic David Hume.

SIGNIFICANT WORK

Natural Theology or *Evidences of the Existence and Attributes
    of the Deity* (1802);
A View of the Evidences of Christianity (1794).

C. S. Lewis (1898–1963)

BACKGROUND

Clive Staples Lewis was an Oxford University professor and a former atheist. He was well known for his radio broadcast in England during World War II that covered many issues related to Christianity and apologetics. He was a brilliant and creative writer and communicator. His books not only covered Christian apologetics, but also fiction and literature.

CLASSIFICATION

Classical Apologetics

APOLOGETICS

Lewis agreed with classical arguments for the existence of God, but he devoted most of his attention to the moral argument. He argued that there must be an objective moral law or no ethical judgments would make sense. You could never call anything evil or wrong if there was no objective moral law. Since the moral law is more like mind than matter, there must be a Mind who is a moral lawgiver to account for it. Lewis also defended the possibility and actuality of miracles and developed an answer to the problem of Evil and pain. He argued that naturalism (belief that all is matter) was self-contradictory and ignored the fact that there is more than nature. Evil, he argued, is a corruption of good that arose from human free choice. God only permits evil when there is a good purpose, even though we may not know what purpose it serves.

SIGNIFICANT WORKS

Mere Christianity;
Miracles;
The Problem of Pain;
The Abolition of Man.

Francis Schaeffer (1912–1984)

BACKGROUND

Francis Schaeffer was born in Germantown, Pennsylvania. He studied at Hampden-Sydney College and Westminster Seminary. At Sydney College he studied under Cornelius Van Til. After graduating, he spent ten years in the United States as a pastor. He then went with his wife,

Edith, to Switzerland as a missionary in 1948. There he left the mission board, and started L'Abri Fellowship as an outreach to British and American college students. His ministry became known as an intellectual critique that challenged cultural influences.

CLASSIFICATION
Presuppositional

APOLOGETICS
Schaeffer considered himself an evangelist or pre-evangelist. His earliest apologetic works were given as lectures. He was not systematic in his approach. He provided excellent critiques of contemporary cultural expressions of irrationalism, subjectivism, and existentialism. His apologetics begins with the presumed truth of the triune God and the Bible. From there, he would use the common ground of creation, morality, and reason to appeal to unbelievers. He also appealed to the pragmatic problem of systems of thought apposed to Christianity. He emphasized the unity and consistency of Christianity. Although, his approach did not rely on arguments for God, he did acknowledge some aspects of the cosmological argument.

SIGNIFICANT WORKS
The God who is There (1968);
Escape from Reason (1968);
He Is There and He Is Not Silent (1972);
Genesis in Space and Time (1972);
How Shall We Then Live (1976);
Whatever Happened to the Human Race? (1979).

Norman L. Geisler

BACKGROUND
Norman Geisler was born in Detroit, Michigan and graduated from Wheaton College and William Tyndale College. In 1972 he graduated from the Ph.D. program in philosophy from Loyola University, a Catholic Jesuit school. A protestant evangelical scholar, Geisler has served nine years as a pastor and over forty years as a professor at various schools including Trinity Evangelical Divinity School, Dallas Theological Seminary, and Liberty University. In 1992 he co-founded

Southern Evangelical Seminary that specializes in programs that deal with apologetics and in 2009 co-founded Veritas Evangelical Seminary. He has authored numerous books on apologetics and theology and has debated others on many positions opposed to the Christian faith.

CLASSIFICATION
Classical Apologetics

APOLOGETICS
Geisler's approach to apologetics is not only classical but can also be described as Thomistic (in the tradition of Aquinas' philosophy). His approach to arguing for Christianity involves three steps. First, he examines various methods of knowing truth (epistemology) that relies exclusively on rationality, empirical fact, practicality, and experience. In place of these he presents unaffirmablity (self-defeating statements) and undeniability (statements that cannot be denied) as the only two adequate tests for truth. Second, he builds his case for Theism (God) on the cosmological argument. It is grounded on a first principle of thought that begins with existence (or being, that is "something exists"). Since this statement is undeniable an argument for Theism is achievable that passes the test for truth. Hence, Theism alone is true and all other views opposed to it are false. The God of Theism is identifiable as the God of Christianity. Third, the case for Christianity can be argued based on historical analysis that includes the reliability of the Bible and the resurrection of Jesus Christ.

SIGNIFICANT WORKS
General Introduction to the Bible (1968, 1986);
Philosophy of Religion (1974, 1987);
Christian Apologetics (1976);
When Skeptics Ask (1990);
Baker Encyclopedia of Apologetics (1999).

DIGITAL OR TRANSPARENCY MASTERS

APOLOGETICS . . .

. . . is the application of

knowledge

to demonstrate that Christianity

is true

TASKS OF APOLOGETICS

TRUTH OF CHRISTIANITY
QUESTIONS ABOUT . . .
BIBLE   JESUS CHRIST

EXISTENCE OF GOD
QUESTIONS ABOUT . . .
GOD MIRACLES EVIL WORLD VIEW

PHILOSOPHICAL FOUNDATION
QUESTIONS ABOUT . . .
TRUTH KNOWLEDGE SELF-EVIDENT TRUTH

CHAPTER 1 REVIEW
"THE NEED TO ANSWER EVERY MAN"

NAME_____

SCORE_____

Directions: Answer the following questions based on your reading of chapter 1.

1. Which individual (young man or Pastor) best describes your experience with arguments and evidences for Christianity? Explain your answer.

   _____
   _____
   _____
   _____
   _____

2. Describe the different ministries of evangelism and pre-evangelism.

   _____
   _____
   _____
   _____
   _____

3. Give three simple reasons why we need to be involved in pre-evangelism.

   _____
   _____
   _____
   _____
   _____

4. Identify what is wrong with each supposed objection to doing pre-evangelism.

    "Do not Answer a Fool . . . (Proverbs 26:4)

    _____

    _____

    "Logic is not valid . . .

    _____

    _____

    "Pre-evangelism was not done in the Bible . . .

    _____

    _____

ASSIGNMENT SHEET #1
DISCUSS HOW THE APOLOGETIC AREAS RELATE

NAME_____
SCORE_____

Introduction: In doing apologetics it is often necessary to identify
each objection or question as belonging to one of the three areas of
apologetics. This will help you develop an answer.

Directions: Form teams or groups and think of objections or questions
concerning Christianity. Fill in the chart below with the questions
and objections. Then use the letters and numbers (O1) to classify
each objection or question in the diagram.

Objection to Christianity   Question about Christianity

O1_____   Q1_____

O2_____   Q2_____

O3_____   Q3_____

O4_____   Q4_____

O5_____   Q5_____

O6_____   Q6_____

O7_____   Q7_____

O8_____   Q8_____

ASSIGNMENT SHEET #2
IDENTIFY NEEDS FOR APOLOGETICS IN THE CHURCH
AND COMMUNITY

NAME_____

SCORE_____

Introduction: Everyday we come into contact with people who need answers to questions about truth, God, and Christianity. These are opportunities to use apologetics.

Directions: Listed in the left column below are the three tasks of apologetics. Identify and list people you have come into contact with that may need answers from each task and then identify in the right column what ministry in your church or community may help meet this need by incorporating apologetics.

Task of Apologetic	**Ministry to Incorporate Apologetics**
1. Philosophical Foundation: Truth	
2. Existence of God	
3. Truth of Christianity	

ASSIGNMENT SHEET #3
SOLVE AN APOLOGETIC PROBLEM AS AN INDIVIDUAL

NAME_____

SCORE_____

Introduction: A new neighbor has just moved in across the street from you. In getting to know your neighbor you discover that she does not believe that God exists but would be open to why you believe that God exists.

Directions: Develop a plan and answers to questions about the existence of God.

1.   What passages in the Bible would give you insight concerning this problem?

_____

_____

_____

_____

2.   What persons, books, and ministries could you consult that would help you develop answers to this problem?

_____

_____

_____

_____

3.   What area of apologetics (see Task of Apologetics chart) does this question fall under and how is it related to other areas of apologetics.

_____

_____

_____

_____

_____

4. What are some questions you could ask this person about the problem?

    _____

    _____

    _____

    _____

5. What further questions or areas do you need to investigate to answer this problem?

    _____

    _____

    _____

    _____

6. What other problems or questions are related and might be asked when you try to answer the question?

    _____

    _____

    _____

    _____

7. How would you go about answering your neighbor's question about God's existence?

    _____

    _____

    _____

    _____

ASSIGNMENT SHEET #4 -SOLVE AN APOLOGETICS PROBLEM IN A GROUP

NAME_____

SCORE_____

Directions: Form teams or groups and use one or more of the following methods to discuss how to answer the question concerning the
existence of God.

A. Group Brainstorming

B. Consulting an Authority or Teacher

C. Role Playing

D. Research

   1. What method(s) of inquiry and discussion did your group
use?

     _____

     _____

     _____

     _____

   2. What were the advantages and disadvantages of addressing the
question as a group?

     _____

     _____

     _____

     _____

   3. What insights were gained by the group that you were unable
to have as an individual?

     _____

     _____

     _____

     _____

INTRODUCTION TO APOLOGETICS
UNIT 1-A

NAME_____
SCORE_____

TEST

I.   Match the terms on the right with their correct definitions.

_____ 1. The study of that which is morally right and wrong.

a. Argument

_____ 2. The study of right reason and valid argumentation.

b. Logic

_____ 3. The belief that one transcendent (separate Being from the Universe) God exists.

c. Truth

d. Apologetics

_____ 4. The love and pursuit of knowledge, beauty, and truth.

e. Philosophy

_____ 5. That which corresponds to reality.

f. Self-evident truth

g. Ethics

_____ 6. Providing a reason for the basis of a conclusion.

h. Theism

_____ 7. The application of knowledge to demonstrate that Christianity is true.

i. Evangelism

j. Bible

_____ 8. The collection of 66 ancient books written under divine inspiration.

k. Faith

_____ 9. Something that is intuitively true and cannot be denied (for example, "I exist" cannot be denied).

_____ 10. Believing something is true based upon the authority of another.

_____ 11. Explaining to another the New Testament Gospel of Jesus Christ.

II.   Match the Task of Apologetics listed on the right with the correct question or objection.

_____   a.   How can there be a good God with evil in the world?

1.   Philosophical Foundation

_____   b.   How do you know the Bible is true?

2.   Existence of God

_____   c.   What is truth?

3.   Truth of Christianity

_____   d.   Miracles are impossible!

_____   e.   What evidence is there for Jesus' resurrection?

III.   Complete the following statements on how the three areas of apologetics relate.

a.   Truth is the _____ to apologetic reasoning.

b.   If truth is possible, then it is possible to give a true argument for the existence of _____.

c.   If God exists, then it is possible to argue that the _____ is His Word.

d.   You must know what kind of question is asked in order to develop an _____.

IV.   Provide answers to each question or statement below.

a.   What is the difference between pre-evangelism and evangelism?

_____
_____
_____

b.   Give two examples of pre-evangelism in the Bible.

_____
_____
_____

c.   Write out 1 Peter 3:15 from memory.

_____
_____
_____

V.   Select true statements concerning the history of apologetics by placing an "X" next to the true statement.

___a. Apologetics was never done in the New Testament.

___b. The Apostle Paul was the only one concerned with apologetics in the New Testament.

___c. Justin Martyr answered objections raised by Gnostics.

___d. Anselm developed the teleological argument.

___e. Thomas Aquinas showed five ways to prove the existence of God.

___f. Blaise Pascal is known for his famous 'wager' argument.

___g. Augustine's most famous apologetic work was the *City of God*.

___h. William Paley developed the teleological argument.

___i. C. S. Lewis converted to Atheism at the end of his life.

___j. Apologetics was never done in the Old Testament.

VI.   Describe the process you would go through if someone asked you a question about Christianity for which you did not know the answer to.

INTRODUCTION TO APOLOGETICS UNIT 1-A

ANSWERS TO TEST

1. f   1.

   B   2.

   E   3.

   G   4.

   D   5.

   I   6.

   A   7.

   C   8.

   K   9.

   H   10.

   J   11.

2. 2   a

   3   b

   1   c

   2   d

   3   e

3. a   foundation

   b   God

   c   Bible

   d   answer

4. a   Pre-evangelism is giving a reason for your faith.

      Evangelism is giving the gospel about Jesus Christ.

   b   Creation account of Genesis 1 and 2.

      Elijah on Mt. Carmel

   c   See 1 Peter 3:15 in the Bible version you are using.

5. c X

   e X

   f X

   g X

   h X

   I X

Answers will vary, but should include investigating related Bible passages, books on the topic, and seeking knowledgeable Christian help.

Appendix C

An Argument for Christianity[1]

REASONING TO CHRISTIANITY
FROM GROUND ZERO

1. There are self-evident truths (e.g., "I exist," "Logic applies to reality").

2. Truth corresponds to reality.

3. Truth is knowable (all other views are self-defeating [chapter 12]).

4. One can proceed from self-evident truths to the existence of God.

    a. The argument from Creation (proceeds from "I exist")

    b. The argument from morals (proceeds from "Values are undeniable")

    c. The argument from design (proceeds from "Design implies a designer")

5. God is a necessary Being (argument from being [chapter 2]).

6. My existence is not necessary (evident from the definition of a necessary Being).

7. Therefore, theism is true (there is a necessary Being beyond the world who has created the contingent things in the world and intervenes in the world [chapter 3]).

    a. The objection from the problem of evil can be solved (chapter 4).

    b. The objection to miracles can be solved (chapter 5).

---

1. Geisler and Brooks, *When Skeptics Ask*, 291–92. Used by Permission. Chapter notations correspond to *When Skeptics Ask*.

8. The Bible is a historically reliable document.

    a. History is an objective study of the past.

    b. There is great historical, archeological, and scientific evidence to confirm the reliability of the Bible (chapters 9–10). (corollary) The Bible gives a reliable record of the teaching of Jesus Christ.

9. Jesus claimed to be both fully human and fully God.

10. He gave evidence to support this claim.

    a. The fulfillment of prophecy

    b. His miraculous and sinless life

    c. His resurrection (chapter 6)

11. Therefore, Jesus is both fully human and fully God.

12. Whatever God teaches is true.

13. Jesus (God) taught that the Old Testament was the inspired Word of God and He promised the New Testament.

14. Therefore, both the Old and New Testaments are the inspired Word of God (chapter 7).

Bibliography

Adler, Mortimer J. *Intellect: Mind over Matter*. New York: Macmillan, 1990.

———. *The Paideia Proposal: An Educational Manifesto*. New York: Macmillian, 1982.

———. *Ten Philosophical Mistakes*. New York: Macmillan, 1985.

Aldrich, Willard M. "Basic Concepts of Bible College Education." *Bibliotheca Sacra* 119 (1962) 244–50.

Anselm, St. *Proslogium; Monologium; An Appendix in Behalf of the Fool by Gaunilon; And Cur Deus Homo*. Translated by Sidney Norton Deane. La Salle, IL: Open Court, 1954.

Aquinas, Thomas. *Summa Contra Gentiles*. Vols. 1–5. Translated by Anton C. Pegis. London: Notre Dame, 1975.

———. *The Summa Theologica of St. Thomas Aquinas*. Vols. 1–5. Translated by Fathers of the English Dominican Province. Allen, TX: Christian Classics, 1981.

Aristotle, *Nicomachean Ethics*. In *The Complete Works of Aristotle* vol. 2, edited by Jonathan Barnes. Princeton: Princeton University Press, 1984.

Arndt, William F., and F. Wilbur Gingrich. *A Greek–English Lexicon of the New Testament and Other Early Christian Literature*. 2nd edition. Chicago: University of Chicago Press, 1979.

Augustine. *City of God*. In *Nicene and Post-Nicene Fathers*. 10 Vols, edited by Philip Schaff, 1st Series. 1887 Reprint. Peabody, MA: Hendrickson, 1999.

———. *Concerning Faith of Things Not Seen*. In *Nicene and Post-Nicene Fathers*. 10 Vols, edited by Philip Schaff, 1st Series. 1887 Reprint. Peabody, MA: Hendrickson, 1999.

Barna Research Online. "Teenagers Embrace Religion but are not Excited about Christianity," [article on-line]. Available from: http://www.barna.org/FlexPage .aspx?Page=BarnaUpdateandBarnaUpdateID=45.

Barnard, Leslie W. *Athenagoras: A Study in Second Century Apologetics*. Paris: Beauchesne, 1972.

Barth, Karl *Church Dogmatics*. Vol. 1, *The Doctrine of the Word of God*. 2nd edition. Translated by G. W. Bromiley. Edinburgh: T and T Clark, 1975.

Behe, Michael J. *Darwin's Black Box: The Biochemical Challenge to Evolution*. New York: The Free Press, 1996.

Berger, Kathleen S. *The Developing Person Through the Life Span*. 2nd edition. New York: Worth, 1988.

Berkouwer, G. C. *Holy Scripture*. Translated by Jack Rogers. Grand Rapids: Eerdmans, 1975.

Bloom, Benjamin S., et al. *Taxonomy of Educational Objectives: Handbook I*. New York: MacKay, 1956.

Boa, Kenneth D., and Robert M. Bowman Jr. *Faith has its Reasons: An Integrative Approach to Defending Christianity*. Colorado Springs: NavPress, 2001.

Bowman, Robert M, Jr. *Orthodoxy and Heresy: A Biblical Guide to Doctrinal Discernment.* Grand Rapids: Baker, 1992.

Brown, Michael L. *Answering Jewish Objections to Jesus.* 3 Vols. Grand Rapids: Baker, 2000–2003.

Brush, Nigel. *The Limitations of Scientific Truth.* Grand Rapids: Kregel, 2005.

Bultmann, Rudolf. *What is Theology?* Translated by Roy A. Harrisville. Minneapolis: Fortress, 1997.

Bush, L. Russ. *A Handbook for Christian Philosophy.* Grand Rapids: Zondervan, 1991.

Butler, Joseph. *Analogy of Religion, Natural and Revealed.* New York: Harper and Brothers, 1870.

Calvin, John. *Institutes of the Christian Religion.* Translated by Henry Beveridge. Grand Rapids: Eerdmans, 1989.

Carnell, Edward J. *An Introduction to Christian Apologetics.* Grand Rapids: Eerdmans, 1948.

———. *Christian Commitment: An Apologetic.* Grand Rapids: Baker, 1982.

Clabauch, Gary K., and Edward G. Rozycki. *Understanding Schools: the Foundations of Education.* New York: Harper and Row, 1990.

Clark, David K. *Dialogical Apologetics.* Grand Rapids: Baker, 1993.

Clark, Gordon H. *A Christian View of Men and Things.* Grand Rapids: Eerdmans, 1952.

———. *In Defense of Theology.* Milford: Mott Media, 1984.

Clark, Robert E., Lin Johnson, and Allyn K. Sloat, editors. *Christian Education: Foundations for the Future.* Chicago: Moody, 1991.

Corbin, Barney H. "A Thomistic Reply to the Reformed Objection to Natural Theology." *Christian Apologetics Journal* 5 no. 2 (2006) 65–107.

Corduan, Winfried. *Reasonable Faith: Basic Christian Apologetics.* Nashville: Broadman and Holman, 1993.

Craig, William Lane. *The Existence of God & the Beginning of the Universe.* San Bernardino: Here's Life, 1979.

———. *Introduction to Apologetics.* Chicago: Moody, 1984.

———. *The Kalàm Cosmological Argument.* New York: Macmillan, 1979.

Crossan, John D. *Who Killed Jesus?* New York: HarperSanFrancisco, 1995.

Darwin, Charles. *On the Origin of Species.* A Facsimile of the First Edition. Cambridge: Harvard University Press, 1995.

Davis, John J. *Biblical Numerology.* Grand Rapids: Baker, 1968.

Dawkins, Richard. *The God Delusion.* New York: Houghton Mifflin, 2008.

Dennett, Daniel. *Breaking the Spell: Religion as a Natural Phenomenon.* New York: Penguin, 2006.

DeWolf, Harold L. *The Case for Theology in Liberal Perspective.* Philadelphia: Westminster, 1959.

Dulles, Avery Cardinal. *A History of Apologetics.* San Francisco: Ignatius, 2005.

Edge, Findley B. *A History of Christian Education.* Nashville: Broadman and Holman, 1993.

Fletcher, John. *Situation Ethics: The New Morality.* Philadelphia: Westminster, 1966.

Flint, Robert. *Agnosticism.* New York: Charles Scribner's Sons, 1903.

Frame, John M. *Apologetics to the Glory Of God: An Introduction.* Phillipsburg: P & R, 1994.

Frankena, William K. Three *Historical Philosophies of Education: Aristotle, Kant, Dewey.* Keystones of Education Series. Glenview: Scott, Foresman, 1965.

Friesen, Gary, and J. Robin Maxson, *Decision Making and the Will of God*. Eugene: Multnomah, 1980.

Funk, Robert W., et al. *The Acts of Jesus: What Did Jesus Really Do?* New York: HarperCollins, 1998.

Funk, Robert W., Roy W. Hoover, et al. *The Five Gospels: What Did Jesus Really Say?* New York: HarperCollins, 1993.

Gaebelein, Frank E., *The Pattern of God's Truth*. Chicago: Moody, 1968.

Geisler, Norman L., and Abdul Saleeb, *Answering Islam: The Crescent in Light of the Cross*. 2nd edition. Grand Rapids: Baker, 2002.

Geisler, Norman L., and Frank Turek. *I Don't Have Enough Faith to Be an Atheist*. Wheaton: Crossway, 2004.

Geisler, Norman L., and J. Kerby Anderson. *Origin Science: A Proposal for the Creation–Evolution Controversy*. Grand Rapids: Baker, 1987.

Geisler, Norman L., and Paul D. Feinberg, *Introduction to Philosophy: A Christian Perspective*. Grand Rapids: Baker, 1980.

Geisler, Norman L., and Ralph E. MacKenzie, *Roman Catholicism: Agreements and Differences*. Grand Rapids: Baker, 1995.

Geisler, Norman L., and Ron Rhodes. *When Cultists Ask*. Grand Rapids: Baker, 1997.

Geisler, Norman L., and Thomas Howe. *When Critics Ask: A Popular Handbook on Bible Difficulties*. Grand Rapids: Victor, 1992.

Geisler, Norman L., and William E. Nix. *A General Introduction to the Bible*. Chicago: Moody, 1986.

Geisler, Norman L., and William D. Watkins. *Worlds Apart: A Handbook on World Views*. 2nd edition. Grand Rapids: Baker, 1989.

Geisler, Norman L., and Winfried Corduan. *Philosophy of Religion*. 2nd edition. Grand Rapids: Baker, 1988.

Geisler, Norman L. "The Need for Defending the Faith." Southern Evangelical Seminary, http://www.ses.edu/journal/needforapologetics.htm [accessed April 25, 2007]

———. "Some Philosophical Perspectives on Missionary Dialogue," in *Theology and Mission*, edited by David J. Hesselgrave. Grand Rapids: Baker, 1978.

———. *Baker Encyclopedia of Christian Apologetics*. Grand Rapids: Baker, 1999.

———. *Christian Apologetic*. Grand Rapids, Baker, 1976.

———. *Christian Ethics*. Grand Rapids, Baker, 1987.

———. *Miracles and the Modern Mind: A Defense of Biblical Miracles*. Grand Rapids: Baker, 1992.

———. *Thomas Aquinas: An Evangelical Appraisal*. Grand Rapids: Baker, 1991.

———. *Apologetics in Christian Educational Ministry* [Class Notes, Charlotte, NC: Southern Evangelical Seminary, 2002].

———. *Systematic Theology*. 4 Vols. Minneapolis: Bethany House, 2002–2005.

Gilson, Etienne. "Can the Existence of God Still be Demonstrated?" In *The McAuley Lectures, 1960*. West Harford, CT: Saint Joseph College, 1960.

———. *Methodical Realism*. Front Royal, VA: Christendom, 1990.

———. "The Eminence of Teaching." In *Disputed Questions in Education*. New York: Doubleday, 1954.

Grotius, Hugo. *The Truth of the Christian Religion*. London: William Baynes, 1829.

Habermas, Gary R. *The Resurrection of Jesus*. Grand Rapids: Baker, 1980.

Hackett, Stuart C. *The Resurrection of Theism*. 2nd edition. Grand Rapids: Baker, 1982.

Hagopian, David G., editor. *The Genesis Debate: Three Views on the Days of Creation.* Mission Viejo: Crux, 2001.

Hanegraaff, Hank. *Christianity in Crisis.* Eugene: Harvest House, 1993.

Harris, Sam. *The End of Faith: Religion, Terror, and Future of Reason.* New York: W. W. Norton, 2004.

———. *Letter to a Christian Nation.* New York: Random House, 2006.

Henry, Carl F. H. *God Revelation, and Authority.* 6 Vols. Waco: Word, 1976–1983.

Hitchens, Christopher. *God Is Not Great: How Religion Poisons Everything.* New York: Hachette, 2007.

Hick, John. *A Christian Theology of Religions.* Louisville: Westminster John Knox, 1995.

Howe, Frederic R. *Challenge and Response: A Handbook of Christian Apologetics.* Grand Rapids: Zondervan, 1982.

Howe, Richard. [*AP10 Problems in Apologetics Class Notes*, Southern Evangelical Seminary, Charlotte, NC, 1997].

Howe, Thomas A. "Practical Hermeneutics: How to Interpret Your Bible Correctly (Part Two)." *Christian Research Journal* 26 (2003) 26–31.

Howe, Thomas A. *Objectivity in Biblical Interpretation.* Altamonte Springs: Advantage, 2004.

Hume, David. *Dialogues Concerning Natural Religion.* Indianapolis: Hackett, 1985.

———. *Enquiries Concerning Human Understanding and Concerning the Principles of Morals.* 3rd edition. New York: Clarendon, 1992.

Inhelder, Bärbel, and Jean Piaget. *The Growth of Logical Thinking From Childhood to Adolescence: An Essay on the Construction of Formal Operational Structures.* Translated by Anne Parsons and Stanley Milgram. France: Basic, 1958.

Johnson, James A., et al. *Introduction to the Foundations of American Education.* 9th edition. Boston: Allyn and Bacon, 1994.

Joy, Donald M., *Moral Development Foundations: Judeo-Christian Alternatives to Piaget/Kohlberg.* Nashville: Abingdon, 1983.

Justin Martyr, *The First Apology of Justin.* In *The Ante-Nicene Fathers.* 10 Vols, edited by Alexander Roberts and James Donaldson. Grand Rapids: Eerdmans, 1979.

———. *The Second Apology of Justin.* In *The Ante-Nicene Fathers.* 10 Vols, edited by Alexander Roberts and James Donaldson. Grand Rapids: Eerdmans, 1979.

Kant, Immanuel. *Critique of Pure Reason.* Translated by Werner S. Pluhar. Indianapolis: Hackett, 1996.

Kantzer, Kenneth Sealer. "John Calvin's Theory of the Knowledge of God and the Word of God." PhD thesis, Harvard University, 1950.

Kennedy, Leonard A., editor. *Thomistic Papers IV.* Houston: The Center for Thomistic Studies, 1988.

Kierkegaard, Søren. *Concluding Unscientific Postscript to Philosophical Fragments.* Vol. 1. Translated by Howard V. and Edna H. Hong. Princeton: Princeton University Press, 1985.

Knight, George R. *Philosophy and Education: An Introduction in Christian Perspective.* Berrien Springs, MI: Andrews University Press, 1980.

Knowles, Malcolm S. *The Adult Learner: A Neglected Species.* 2nd edition. Houston: Gulf, 1978.

Kohlberg, Lawrence. *The Philosophy of Moral Development: Moral Stages and the Idea of Justice.* Vol. 1. New York: Harper and Row, 1981.

Kosmin, Barry A., Egon Mayar, and Ariela Keysar. "American Religious Identification Survey 2001 The Graduate Center of the City University of New York," 2001. http://www.gc.cuny.edu/faculty/research_briefs/aris.pdf [accessed May 17, 2007].

Kreeft, Peter, and Ronald K. Tacelli. *A Handbook of Christian Apologetics.* Colorado Springs: NavPress, 1997.

LaBar, Louis E. *Education That is Christian.* Old Tappan: Revell, 1958.

Laska, John A. *Schooling and Education: Basic Concepts and Problems.* New York: Nostrand, 1976.

Lewis, C. S. *The Abolition of Man.* New York: Macmillan, 1986.

———. *God in the Dock: Essays on Theology and Ethics,* edited by Walter Hooper. Grand Rapids: Eerdmans, 1970.

———. *The Great Divorce.* New York: Macmillan, 1946.

———. *Mere Christianity.* New York: Macmillan, 1952.

———. *Miracles.* New York: Macmillan, 1978

———. *The Problem of Pain.* New York: Macmillan, 1986.

———. *The Weight of Glory.* New York: Collier, 1980.

Lewis, Gordon R. *Testing Christianity's Truth Claims.* New York: University Press of America, 1990.

Mager, Robert F. *Preparing Instructional Objectives.* 2nd edition. Belmont, CA: Fearon, 1962.

Magevney, Eugene. *Christian Education in the First Centuries.* New York: Reprint, 1898; The Cathedral Library Association, 1900.

Maritain, Jacques. *On the Philosophy of History.* Clifton, NJ: Kelley, 1973.

Martin, Michael. *Atheism: A Philosophical Justification.* Philadelphia: Temple University Press, 1990.

———. *The Case Against Christianity.* Philadelphia: Temple University Press, 1991.

Mayers, Ronald B. *Both/And: A Balanced Apologetic.* Chicago: Moody, 1984.

McInerny, Ralph. *A First Glance at St. Thomas Aquinas.* Notre Dame, IN: University of Notre Dame Press, 1990.

McDowell, Josh, and Bob Hostetler. *Beyond Belief to Convictions.* Wheaton: Tyndale, 2002.

———. *Right From Wrong: What You Need to Know to Help Youth Make Right Choices.* Dallas: Word, 1994.

McDowell, Josh. *Evidence That Demands A Verdict.* San Bernardino: Here's Life, 1972.

Miethe, Terry, and Antony Flew. *Does God Exist: A Believer and an Atheist Debate.* New York: HarperSanFrancisco, 1991.

Montgomery, John Warwick. *History and Christianity: A Vigorous, Convincing Presentation of the Evidences for a Historical Jesus.* Minneapolis: Bethany House, 1965.

———. *Tractatus Logico–Theologicus.* Bonn, Germany: Kultur und Wissenschaft, 2002.

Moreland, J. P. *Love Your God with All Your Mind.* Colorado Springs: NavPress, 1997.

———. *Scaling the Secular City.* Grand Rapids: Baker, 1987.

———, editor. *The Creation Hypothesis: Scientific Evidence for an Intelligent Designer.* Downers Grove: InterVarsity, 1994.

Noebel, David A. *Understanding the Times.* Manitou Springs, CO: Summit, 1991.

———. *Understanding The Times.* 2nd edition. Manitou Springs, CO: Summit, 2006.

Origen. "Against Celsus." In *Classical Readings in Christian Apologetics A.D. 100–1800,* edited by L. Russ Bush. Grand Rapids: Zondervan, Academia Books, 1983.

Paley, William A. *View of the Evidences of Christianity*, London: Religious Tract Society, 1853.

Pascal, Blaise. *Pensées*. Translated by A. J. Krailsheimer. New York: Penguin, 1966.

Peterson, Michael L. *Philosophy of Education*. Downers Grove: InterVarsity, 1986.

Pietruski, Glenn. "Comparing Orthodox Christian Doctrine With Select Major Cults: A Teaching Resource." DMin project, Southern Evangelical Seminary, 2008.

Plantinga, Alvin, and Nicholas Wolterstorff, editors. *Faith and Rationality: Reason and Belief in God*. Notre Dame: University of Notre Dame Press, 1983.

Plantinga, Alvin. *Warranted Christian Belief*. New York: Oxford University Press, 2000.

Potter, Douglas E. "Christian Apologetic Education: A Perspective." *The Homeschool Digest*, 13, no. 2 (2002) 39–40.

———. "Humble Apologetics: Defending the Faith Today." Book Review in *Christian Apologetics Journal* 4, no. 2, (2005) 100–103.

———. "Introducing Apologetics: Cultivating Christian Commitment." Book Review in *Christian Apologetics Journal* 8, no. 2, (2009).

———. "The Justification and Implementation of a Christian Apologetics Educational Program at the Secondary School Level." DMin Project, Southern Evangelical Seminary, 2005.

Price, Robert M., and Jeffery Jay Lowder. *The Empty Tomb: Jesus Beyond the Grave*. New York: Prometheus, 2005.

Ramm, Bernard. *Protestant Christian Evidences: A Textbook of the Evidences of the Truthfulness of the Christian faith for Conservative Protestants*. Chicago: Moody, 1953.

Reid, J. K. S. *Christian Apologetics*. Grand Rapids: Eerdmans, 1969.

Rhodes, Ron. *The Culting of America*. Eugene: Harvest, 1994.

Richards, Lawrence O., and Gary J. Bredfeldt. *Creative Bible Teaching*. Revised and expanded edition. Chicago: Moody, 1998.

Rodriguez, Daryl. "Wise As Serpents—Harmless As Doves: Speaking The Truth In Love In A Cultic Age." DMin project, Southern Evangelical Seminary, 2008.

Ross, Hugh. *The Fingerprint of God: Recent Scientific Discoveries Reveal the Unmistakable Identity of the Creator*. 2nd edition. Orlando: Promise, 1989.

———. *The Genesis Question: Scientific Advances and the Accuracy of Genesis*. Colorado Springs: Navpress, 1998.

Schaeffer, Francis A. *The Complete Works of Francis A. Schaeffer*. 5 Vols. 2nd edition. Weschester: Crossway, 1982.

Schaff, Philip. *Post-Nicene Fathers*. 14 Vols. 1st Series Reprint 1887. Peabody, MA: Hendrickson, 1999.

Schleiermacher, Friedrich. *On Religion: Speeches to Its Cultured Despisers*. Louisville: Westminster, 1994.

Sennett, James F., editor. *The Analytical Theist*. Grand Rapids: Eerdmans, 1988.

Smith, George H. *Atheism: The Case Against God*, Buffalo: Prometheus, 1989.

Smith, Henry B. *Introduction to Christian Theology Apologetics*. New York: A. C. Armstrong and Son, 1893.

Snuffer, Ryan P. "Truth In Focus: A Practical Apologetic Textbook For High School Juniors." DMin project, Southern Evangelical Seminary, 2005.

Snuffer, Ryan P. *Truth in Focus: A Practical Defense of the Christian faith for Teens*. Longwood, FL: Xulon Press, 2005.

Scott, David. "A Church without a View: Jonathan Edwards and Our Current Lifeview Discipleship Crisis." *Christian Apologetics Journal* 7, no. 2 (2008) 32–40.

Southern Evangelical Seminary, Catalog 1996–98. Charlotte: Southern Evangelical Seminary, 1996.

———. *Catalog for 1992–93 School Year.* Charlotte: Southern Evangelical Seminary, 1992.

Stackhouse, John G., Jr. *Humble Apologetics: Defending the Faith Today.* Oxford: Oxford University Press, 2002.

Stangner, Frank Bateman. *Spiritual Formation in the Local Church.* Grand Rapids: Zondervan, 1989.

Stoner, Peter W., and Robert C. Newman. *Science Speaks: Scientific Proof of the Accuracy of Prophecy and the Bible.* Chicago: Moody, 1968.

Taylor, James E. *Introducing Apologetics: Cultivating Christian Commitment.* Grand Rapids: Baker, 2006.

Tillich, Paul. *Dynamics of Faith.* New York: Harper, 1957.

Toenges, Scott K. "World Religions And Cults: The Promotion And Implementation Of A Secondary Christian School Curriculum." DMin project, Southern Evangelical Seminary, 2008.

Torrey, R. A., et al., editors. *The Fundamentals: A Testimony to the Truth.* 4 Vols. Reprint. Grand Rapids: Baker, 1972.

Vacca, Richard T., and Jo Anne L. Vacca, *Content Area Reading.* 3rd edition. Glenview: Scott, Foresman, 1989.

Van Til, Cornelius. *The Defense of the Faith.* Phillipsburg, NJ: Presbyterian and Reformed, 1967.

Warfield, Benjamin B. *The Works of Benjamin B. Warfield.* Vol. 9, *The Idea of Systematic Theology.* Oxford: 1932. Reprint, Grand Rapids: Baker, 2003.

Warren, Jeffrey L. "Training Youth Workers to Teach Youth Basic Christian Apologetics." DMin project, Southwestern Baptist Theological Seminary, 1995. Text–fiche.

Watchman Fellowship, Inc. "Watchman Fellowship's 2001 Index of Cults and Religions" [data on–line]. Available from: http://www.watchman.org/cat95.htm.

Wilhelmsen, Frederick D. *Man's Knowledge of Reality: An Introduction to Thomistic Epistemology.* Englewood Cliffs: Prentice–Hall, 1956.

Wilson, Clifford A. *Rocks, Relics and Biblical Reliability.* Grand Rapids: Zondervan, 1982.

Zacharias, Ravi, and Norman Geisler, editors. *Is Your Church Ready? Motivating Leaders to Live an Apologetic Life.* Grand Rapids: Zondervan, 2003.

———. *Who Made God? And Answers to Over 100 Other Tough Questions of Faith.* Grand Rapids: Zondervan, 2003.

Zuck, Roy B. *Teaching as Jesus Taught.* Grand Rapids: Baker, 1995.

———. *The Holy Spirit in Your Teaching.* Revised edition. Wheaton: Victor, 1984.